THE LO**** ****
*Selected Poems*

RUDYARD KIPLING was born in Bombay in 1865, where his father taught at the government school of art. In 1871, he and his even younger sister were sent back to England to live with a family called the Holloways, a time of his life he always remembered as deeply unhappy. After attending United Services College in Devon, he returned to India in 1882 to become a journalist in Lahore, later moving to Allahabad. His experiences during this period provided the material for the poems and stories that were published as *Departmental Ditties* (1886) and *Plain Tales from the Hills* (1888). In 1889 Kipling returned to England, publishing *Barrack-Room Ballads* in 1892, the year in which he married and moved to Vermont, where he lived until 1896. In addition to his prolific career as a prose writer, Kipling produced several more collections of verse, most notably *The Seven Seas* (1896), *The Five Nations* (1903) and *The Years Between* (1919). In 1902 he settled at Bateman's in Sussex with his family, although he continued to travel widely. In 1907 he became the first English writer to receive the Nobel Prize for literature. He died in 1936.

HARRY RICKETTS was born in London in 1950 and is Associate Professor in the English Department of Victoria University of Wellington, New Zealand. He is the author of *The Unforgiving Minute: A Life of Rudyard Kipling* (1999) and seven collections of poetry.

Fyfield*Books* aim to make available some of the great classics of British and European literature in clear, affordable formats, and to restore often neglected writers to their place in literary tradition.

Fyfield*Books* take their name from the Fyfield elm in Matthew Arnold's 'Scholar Gypsy' and 'Thyrsis'. The tree stood not far from the village where the series was originally devised in 1971.

> *Roam on! The light we sought is shining still.*
> *Dost thou ask proof? Our tree yet crowns the hill,*
> *Our Scholar travels yet the loved hill-side*

from 'Thyrsis'

RUDYARD KIPLING

# The Long Trail
*Selected Poems*

Edited with an introduction by
HARRY RICKETTS

FyfieldBooks

CARCANET

First published in Great Britain in 2004 by
Carcanet Press Limited
Alliance House
Cross Street
Manchester M2 7AQ

A CIP catalogue record for this book is available from the British Library
ISBN 1 85754 739 X

The publisher acknowledges financial assistance from Arts Council England

Typeset by XL Publishing Services, Tiverton
Printed and bound in England by SRP Ltd, Exeter

# Contents

# Introduction

'What were the white people like in the places you stayed at in the tropics?' ...

'Some of them,' he said, 'were rather like composite characters out of Conrad and Kipling.'

That was how Siegfried Sassoon later recalled the opening of his one brief tête à tête with Rupert Brooke in early July 1914. Brooke had just returned from a year in America and the Pacific, and Sassoon – at that stage still rather more foxhunting man than poet – was trying to engage him in conversation. Picking up on the reference to Kipling, Sassoon dismissed his poetry as 'terribly tub-thumping stuff'. To his surprise, Brooke demurred ('But not always, surely'), before adding considerately: 'I used to think rather the same myself until Eddie [Marsh] made me read *Cities and Thrones and Powers*. There aren't many better modern poems than that, you know.'[1]

In fact, as Sassoon admitted many years later when he wrote up his encounter with Brooke, his antipathy to Kipling's poetry was not nearly as strong as he had made out. He was fond enough of 'The Return of the Children', for instance, to know the opening lines by heart:

Neither the harps nor the crowns amused, nor the cherubs'
dove-winged races –
Holding hands forlornly the Children wandered beneath the
Dome,
Plucking the splendid robes of the passers-by, and with pitiful
faces
Begging what Princes and Powers refused: – 'Ah, please will
you let us go home?'

---

1  Siegfried Sassoon, *The Weald of Youth* (London: Faber and Faber, 1942), 229. Parts of this introduction were delivered (in a different form and context) as a paper on Kipling's literary afterlife at the Kipling Conference held at Magdalene College, Cambridge in September 2001.

Which is an interesting concession as far as it goes. But, looking back, it never seems to have occurred to Sassoon that the poet he so glibly disparaged to Brooke could have exerted a significant influence on his own work – on the angry, adhesive anti-war poems he wrote only a couple of years later. It plainly never crossed his mind that poems like '"Blighters"', '"They"', 'Base Details' and 'In the Pink' were descendants of Kipling's 'Tommy' ('But it's "Thin red line of 'eroes" when the drums begin to roll'), 'The Widow at Windsor' ('(Poor beggars! – it's blue with our bones!)'), and 'The Young British Soldier' ('Jest roll to your rifle and blow out your brains').

Sassoon could recognise, and acknowledge, the influence of Hardy's 'satires of circumstance', but not that of Kipling's 'barrack-room ballads'. At the time Sassoon was writing the poems (1916–18), it is easy to see why. For him, Kipling would have meant the bellicose conscriptionist of '"For All We Have and Are"' ('Stand up and take the war./The Hun is at the Gate!'), not the devastated father of 'My Boy Jack' ('"Have you any news of my boy Jack?"/*Not this tide.*'). It would have been impossible for Sassoon, committed to his brave protest against the war, to imagine a Kipling engaged in his own form of poetic 'counter-attack'. But he was. His 'Epitaphs of the War' sequence contains poems as bitter and bleakly compassionate as anything in Sassoon. 'Common Form' shows a Kipling – his son died at Loos in 1915 – who counts himself among the lying fathers: 'If any question why we died,/Tell them, because our fathers lied.' 'Unknown Female Corpse' reaches beyond the entrenched polarities of ally and enemy to a shared vision of horror and a shared humanity:

> Headless, lacking foot and hand,
> Horrible I come to land.
> I beseech all women's sons
> Know I was a mother once.

This Kipling has a good deal in common with Sassoon, and is the same Kipling whose 'Dirge of Dead Sisters' Vera Brittain used to chant to keep herself going in July 1916 as a VAD in the 1st London General Hospital, Camberwell:

> (When the days were torment and the nights were clouded
>                                                      terror
>     When the Powers of Darkness had dominion on our soul –

When we fled consuming through the Seven Hells of Fever,
These put out their hands to us and healed and made us
whole.)

This Kipling, speaking for the desperate and the dead, has been too often forgotten or ignored – so much more convenient to dismiss him as writing 'terribly tub-thumping stuff'.

When Brooke told Sassoon that some of the 'white men' he encountered in the Pacific were 'rather like composite characters out of Conrad and Kipling', he was simply reiterating a motif from his recent letters to friends. 'It is all incredibly like a Kipling story,' he told Eddie Marsh in November 1913 en route from Samoa to Fiji, '& all the [white] people are very self-consciously Kiplingesque.' Which shows how quickly the term Kiplingesque had taken root. And, to judge by another letter the same month, the term already carried for liberal readers an uncomfortable cargo of imperialist associations. 'One feels that one's a White Man – ludicrously,' Brooke wrote Edmund Gosse, adding with an asterisk: 'Vide R. Kipling *passim*.'[2]

Brooke could see the ludicrousness; he could also appreciate a poem like 'Cities and Thrones and Powers'. Sassoon's reaction, however, proved more characteristic of how the literary world continued to respond to Kipling. Throughout the twentieth century, he remained the literary ancestor few major writers were prepared to acknowledge openly – and then only grudgingly or half-heartedly. Joyce admitted that the general plan of *Dubliners* was taken from *Plain Tales from the Hills*, but it took Edmund Wilson to point out that Joyce 'would never have written the Cyclops chapter of *Ulysses*, if he had never read Kipling'.[3] Hemingway admitted, reluctantly and back-handedly, to the influence of 'the good Kipling'. Even T.S. Eliot, whose *A Choice of Kipling's Verse* (1941) with its magisterial introduction did much to restore Kipling's standing as a poet, was stingy in his own attributions. He merely conceded that two of his titles owed a debt to two of Kipling's: 'The Love Song of J Alfred Prufrock' to 'The Love Song of Har Dyal' and 'The Hollow Men' to 'The Broken Men'. No mention of Kipling's obvious influence on the Cockney

2  Geoffrey Keynes (ed.), *The Letters of Rupert Brooke* (London: Faber and Faber, 1968), 526, 531.
3  Edmund Wilson, 'Kipling's *Debits and Credits*', *New Republic*, 6 October 1926.

pub scene in part two of *The Waste Land*. No mention that the laughter-containing children, hidden in the leaves in the first section of 'Burnt Norton', were refugees from Kipling's story '"They"'. No mention that the metre of 'Skimbleshanks' was lifted straight from 'The Long Trail' and that of 'Growltiger's Last Stand' from 'The Glory of the Garden'.[4]

In fact, once one starts to look for them, Kipling's fingerprints are smudged all over twentieth-century literature. They are there in Anthony Powell's depictions of school and Army life in *A Dance to the Music of Time* (Stringham's 'Braddock alias Thorne' hoax is pure Stalky; Captain Gwatkin tries unsuccessfully to model himself on 'A Song of Mithras' from *Puck of Pook's Hill*.) They are there in Evelyn Waugh's *Sword of Honour* trilogy, Waugh's officers almost involuntarily breaking into quotations from Kipling: '"A woman's only a woman but a good cigar is a smoke," said the major'; '"The captains and the kings depart," said de Souza.' In a typically cruel, and funny, manoeuvre, Waugh even has Colonel Ritchie-Hook (an uncharmed version of Stalky) slightly misquote 'If –': 'Even after you win your battle, you're never the same again. There are reinforcements and promotions. You have to "start all over again from your beginnings, and never breathe a word about your loss." Isn't that how the poem goes?'[5] Well, not quite, replies the alert reader (perhaps one of those who in 1995 overwhelmingly voted 'If-' the UK's favourite poem). The lines should read: 'And lose, and *start again* at your beginnings / And never breathe a word about your loss' (My italics).

As in fiction, so in life. When General Wavell comprehensively defeated the Italian forces in Egypt at Beda Fomm in early 1941, he received the following telegram: 'The Kipling Society sends congratulations on Tabaqui's discomfiture and all good wishes.' To which the General fittingly replied: 'Many thanks. Hope Shere Khan's skin will soon be on Council Rock.' Over sixty years on, we

4 Craig Raine, *Rudyard Kipling: Selected Poetry* (London: Penguin, 1992), xxiii, xxv. Raine's introduction offers the most concerted case for Kipling's qualities as a poet. He shows Kipling to have been an often extremely subtle metricist and emphatically answers the charge that Kipling 'writes terrific tunes but misses out on melody'. Raine also persuasively argues for Kipling the poet to be thought of as 'a modernist rather than the dated Edwardian of conventional criticism'.
5 Evelyn Waugh, *Unconditional Surrender* (London: Chapman and Hall, 1961), 204, 290; *Men At Arms* (London: Penguin, 1964), 70.

still have no problem translating the code, reading Mussolini for Tabaqui and Hitler for Shere Khan. Nor, like Montgomery's subordinates, do we have any trouble decoding the 'Good hunting' with which the General used to end his orders for the day.[6]

A more unexpected set of Kipling's fingerprints shows up in the work of the Marxist poet and playwright Bertolt Brecht. Brecht translated and imitated several of Kipling's poems (including 'If –') and was one of those who did acknowledge his debt: 'Additional ballads by Villon and Kipling' reads the original 1928 programme of *The Threepenny Opera*. At first, it may seem odd that Kipling could have had anything to offer a writer with such radically different political beliefs. But only if one forgets Kipling's lifelong sympathy and admiration for 'the 3rd class carriages'.[7] Which is presumably why the left-wing, working-class protest singer Billy Bragg chose to record 'A Pict Song' (from *Puck of Pook's Hill*) on his 1996 album *William Bloke*, Kipling's words perfectly catching what it feels like to be a member of an underclass, desperate and oppressed.

Another poet whose early work (at least) offers a clear set of Kipling's prints is W.H. Auden. Again the politics may initially seem different, but the panoramic view, urgent warning, fascination with machinery, and hectoring note of these thumping couplets from 1930 strongly recall poems like Kipling's 'The Islanders':

Get there if you can and see the land you once were proud to
own
Though the roads have almost vanished and the expresses
never run ...
Head-gears gaunt on grass-grown pit-banks, seams
abandoned long ago;
Drop a stone and listen for its splash in flooded dark below ...
Far from there we spent the money, thinking we could well
afford,
While they quietly undersold us with their cheaper trade
abroad ...
If we really want to live, we'd better start at once to try;
If we don't it doesn't matter, but we'd better start to die.

6  Kipling Papers 28/14, Sussex University Library.
7  Thomas Pinney (ed.), *The Letters of Rudyard Kipling, Volume 2: 1890–1899* (London: Macmillan, 1990), 306.

'It is later than you think' warns the speaker of Auden's 'Consider this and in our time' (also 1930); the very words Kipling had inscribed on the sundial at his house in Sussex.[8]

Then there is the strange case of 'In Memory of W.B. Yeats'. Auden wrote the elegy in early 1939 in the immediate aftermath of Yeats's death. The third section contains the stanzas:

Time that is intolerant
Of the brave and innocent,
And indifferent in a week
To a beautiful physique,

Worships language and forgives
Everyone by whom it lives;
Pardons cowardice, conceit,
Lays its honours at their feet.

Time that with this strange excuse
Pardoned Kipling and his views,
And will pardon Paul Claudel,
Pardons him for writing well.[9]

Not only does the still left-wing Auden pardon the recently dead right-wing Kipling, but he does so very appropriately with a subtle echo of the third stanza of the poem Brooke commended to Sassoon, 'Cities and Thrones and Powers' – itself a rather bleaker elegy than Auden's on the vanity of human wishes:

Time that is o'er-kind,
To all that be
Ordains us e'en as blind,
As bold as she:
That in our very death,
And burial sure,
Shadow to shadow, well-persuaded saith,
'See how our works endure!'

8  Edward Mendelson (ed.), *The English Auden: Poems, Essays and Dramatic Writings 1927–1939* (London: Faber and Faber, 1986, paperback edition), 48–9, 47.
9  *The English Auden*, 242–3. In later years, Auden dropped the Kipling stanza: either because he decided Time had not pardoned Kipling after all or, more likely, because he thought the introduction of Kipling (and Claudel) deflected attention from Yeats, the subject of his elegy.

A year before he (and Time) pardoned 'Kipling and his views', Auden edited the *Oxford Book of Light Verse*. There he was less merciful, describing Kipling in his introduction as a writer of 'serious light verse' and then, peculiarly, representing him by a single entry, 'Danny Deever'.[10] There is, of course, nothing inherently damning about the designation 'serious light verse'; Auden wrote much himself, including 'Miss Gee', 'As I walked out one evening' and 'Under Which Lyre'. But what Auden did was debar Kipling from being seen as a writer of *un*serious light verse, a descendant of Praed and Calverley, the author of such neatly judged pieces as 'The Pious Sub's Creed' and 'A Code of Morals' – not to mention the best of the parodies in *Echoes* (1884) and 'The Muse Among the Motors' (c.1901–29). Auden's label continued a process of erasure which dated back to the Boer War and Kipling's stridently pro-British stance. (Which was what really did for him and his reputation in liberal and literary circles.) Max Beerbohm's famous 1904 cartoon damningly made the point. A diminutive Kipling, hanging on the arm of a large, disinterested Britannia, frantically blows his toy trumpet. He wears her helmet, she his bowler. The caption, mimicking Kipling's use of Cockney, reads: 'Mr Rudyard Kipling takes a bloomin' day aht, on the blasted 'eath, along with Britannia, 'is gurl.' After that, Kipling could be – often was – a butt; he could no longer be fun. As a result, the lighter Kipling (like the compassionate Kipling and the lyrical Kipling) continues to be discounted and disregarded. And yet traces of all three can be detected not only in Auden's work but in that of three of his most engaging and readily quotable heirs, Gavin Ewart, James Fenton and Wendy Cope.

George Orwell, an admirer (like Auden) well this side of idolatry, used to enjoy pointing out that Kipling was so memorable that he was often quoted unconsciously. 'Nothing', wrote Orwell, 'could exceed the contempt of the *New Statesman*, for instance, for Kipling, but many times during the Munich period did the *New Statesman* find itself quoting that phrase about paying the Danegeld?' In a subsequent note to his essay, Orwell also cited a prize example of Kipling's lines being unconsciously reattributed to a more 'respectable' author:

10 W.H. Auden (ed.), *W.H. Auden's Oxford Book of Light Verse* (Oxford: Oxford University Press, 1938), xviii–xix (footnote).

On the first page of his recent book *Adam and Eve*, Mr Middleton Murry quotes the well-known lines:

> There are nine and sixty ways
> Of constructing tribal lays,
> And every single one of them is right.

He attributes these lines to Thackeray. This is what is known as a 'Freudian error'. A civilised person would prefer not to quote Kipling, i.e. would prefer not to feel that it was Kipling who had expressed his thought for him.[11]

More farcical versions of such misrememberings abound. One, perhaps apocryphal, involves the Hon. H.L. Tennyson, the rumbustious 1920s cricketing grandson of the Victorian poet. Alan Gibson tells the story in his *The Cricket Captains of England*:

> On one occasion [Tennyson] was bet that he could not write down the names of ten poems written by his grandfather. He managed seven without difficulty, and then, with a bit of a struggle, two more. Finally, after a long pause, he wrote down 'If'. It was pointed out to him that this had been written by Rudyard Kipling. 'Oh', he said 'What *An Absent Minded Beggar* I am.'[12]

A more recent instance, from 1996, concerns Ted Stedman from Hertfordshire, who – at a length of 1.6 metres or 5 foot 2 inches – possessed the longest moustache in the United Kingdom. Asked about the virtues of moustaches, Mr Stedman rakishly replied: 'Someone once said that kissing a man without a moustache is like eating a beef sandwich without mustard.'[13] This is, of course, a splendidly distorted version of an exchange from Kipling's 1888 novella *The Story of the Gadsbys*, in which Emma Deercourt passes on to Minnie Threegan the daring information that '[B]eing kissed … by a man who *didn't* wax his moustache was – like eating an egg without salt.'[14]

11 Andrew Rutherford (ed.), *Kipling's Mind and Art: Selected Critical Essays* (Stanford: Stanford University Press, 1964), 80.
12 Alan Gibson, *The Cricket Captains of England* (London: The Pavilion Library, 1989), 122.
13 Quoted in *The Dominion* (Wellington, New Zealand), 23 November, 1996.
14 *Soldiers Three, The Story of the Gadsbys, In Black and White* (London: Macmillan, 1895), 119.

Less obscure bits of Kipling still constantly crop up in the media and elsewhere. British sports writers still routinely invoke 'Triumph and Disaster' as 'those two impostors' (sometimes misquoted as 'those twin impostors'), and, after the final of the 1998 Soccer World Cup, the BBC wrapped up its coverage with an extended sequence of highlights to a reading of 'If–'. Cricket-haters still disparage the 'flannelled fools'. Commentators on race relations still deplore the notion that 'East is East, and West is West, and never the twain shall meet'. If the runaway Richard Hannay in Hitchcock's 1935 version of *The 39 Steps* can remark in mock-vexation to the girl to whom he is handcuffed: 'You are the White Man's Burden', the police inspector in an episode of a mid-1980s television adaptation of Agatha Christie's *Miss Marple* can observe with equal aplomb to his sergeant: 'You're a better man than I am, Gunga Din!'

In the aftermath of 9/11 and the destruction of the World Trade Towers in New York, it was often Kipling who provided the necessary words. According to *The Daily Telegraph*, one commentator on the day itself quoted the opening of Kipling's 'The Storm Cone' (1932):

This is midnight – let no star
Delude us – dawn is very far.
This is the tempest long foretold,
Slow to make head, but sure to hold.

Robert Fisk, putting events in a larger context a fortnight later in *The Independent*, recalled being a war correspondent in Afghanistan in the 1980s. On a break in Peshawar in Pakistan, he came across an apt verse from 'Arithmetic on the Frontier', framed on the wall of the old Intercontinental Hotel:

A scrimmage at a border station
A canter down a dark defile
Five thousand pounds of education
Felled by a five-rupee jezail.[15]

The term 'Kiplingesque' may now mostly be used in a pejorative sense, but many of Kipling's phrases retain their force and have become simply part of the common currency of the English language.

15 Both of these verses are (perhaps predictably) slightly misquoted.

Variations on the Sassoon–Brooke exchange about Kipling's poetry have been going on for the last ninety years: assumption of mutual antipathy countered by notable exception. One current academic version regularly 'deconstructs' Kipling's work as an A–Z of colonial attitudes. Selected poems and extracts (the opening stanza of 'The White Man's Burden' is a favourite) are chosen to illustrate the idea that, to adapt Sassoon, it is 'terribly empire-thumping stuff'. To which, playing Brooke, one might demur ('But not always, surely'), before adding considerately: 'I used to think rather the same myself until I read 'We and They'. There aren't many better poems about cultural relativity than that, you know.'

# A Note on the Selection and the Text

This new selection of Kipling's poems is arranged chronologically, starting with 'Credat Judaeus', written when he was a fifteen-year-old schoolboy at Westward Ho!, and ending with 'Hymn to Breaking Strain', written within a year of his death at the age of seventy. A chronological ordering may seem a conservative move; in fact, in Kipling's case, it is an almost radical one. Both T.S. Eliot's *A Choice of Kipling's Verse* (1941) and Craig Raine's *Rudyard Kipling: Selected Poetry* (1992) – the two best-known and most influential twentieth-century selections of the poems – jump around without any apparent logic. It seems worth offering readers the opportunity to sample Kipling from early to late.

Apart from novelty, the chronological approach has the advantage that readers at once encounter a less familiar (for some, even an unknown) Kipling – the precocious heir of the Brownings and the Pre-Raphaelites, and the witty adapter of Horace. After the early accomplishment of 'Credat Judaeus' and 'Overheard', later dramatic monologues like 'A Vision of Hamid Ali', 'One Viceroy Resigns' and the great 'McAndrew's Hymn' seem less of a surprise, more like one of several natural progressions. After 'An Auto-da-Fé', the many subsequent lyrics of loss and stoical acceptance like 'The Harp Song of the Dane Women', 'My Boy Jack' and 'Hymn to Physical Pain' seem much less unexpected. If 'Ave Imperatrix!' clearly anticipates the imperial rhetoric and cadence of 'Recessional', the playful ventriloquism of 'Donec Gratus Eram' equally clearly looks forward to the confident demotic of the 'Barrack-Room Ballads' and to the underrated poetic parodies in *Echoes* and 'The Muse Among the Motors'.

Another advantage of reading Kipling chronologically is testing out the often repeated assertion that he never developed. In terms of technique, the claim is true – up to a point. Although he rarely strayed into free verse (but see 'The Galley-Slaves') and only occasionally tackled the tougher traditional forms (but see 'Sestina of the Tramp-Royal'), Kipling was very much more than a metrical thumper, forever banging out the same tune. The sound and rhythmic effects in the poems can be wonderfully subtle and delicate, as Craig Raine and others have demonstrated. What is patently untrue is that the emotional range and depth in the poems never developed. The later lyrics and epitaphs are shot through with personal feeling, including compassion for those who suffer.

This selection provides, I hope, a more lyrical, a more playful, a more meditative Kipling than the one usually on show. Of course, there is a decent round-up of the 'usual suspects' – I have not tried to erase the music-hall bard of 'Mandalay', the empire laureate of 'The White Man's Burden' or the belligerent patriot of 'For All We Have and Are' – but I have tried to summon other less predictable but equally characteristic Kiplings to this poetic identity parade.

For the text of the poems, I have generally followed that of the *Definitive Edition* (and for the early work that of Andrew Rutherford's *Early Verse of Rudyard Kipling 1879–1889*). In a few instances, I have silently corrected obvious typographical errors and standardised the punctuation. Dates and epigraphs below the titles of the poems are Kipling's own. There are brief editorial notes at the back of the book.

Harry Ricketts
September 2003

# Credat Judaeus

Three couples were we in the lane,
Keeping our walks and turning again;
    At the point where we meet
    The roar of the street
Like the sound of a beast in pain
    Comes faintly. Here all is sweet.

Who were the others? I did not see.
    Why should I look at the men at all?
Why should their partners interest me?
    I'm sure that I loved mine best of all.

    Perfect in beauty and grace,
    Perfect in figure and face,
She with her eyes divine!
    The present for just us two;
Eternity makes her mine,
    *Our* love is eternal and true!

SECOND COUPLE

Watch them, dearest, cheek to cheek,
    Arm in arm; when years are past
    Will their love like our love last,
Still so fond, still cheek to cheek?

There is one true love below;
    We have found it! Others kiss
    For a little, part and miss,
Grieve awhile, then lightly go.

These in earnest! I have seen
    Many such; the years will fly,
    Leave us loving, you and I,
While they talk of what has been.

I wanted them walks so bad
With you, and missus is mad
'Cos she says I gad out at night;
No doubt but what she's right.

Well, I can't stay long, but see,
Promise to 'old to me,
    An I'll 'old to you for hever!
Them people may court a bit –
    They don't love like we two!
    Oh, George! I've got no one but you.
'Old by me! Promise it!
    And I'll never leave you, never!

I, the writer that made them speak,
    Laughed aloud as I passed the three,
Strong in a passion to last a week,
    For Love that is real was given to me!


## An Auto-da-Fé


And did you love me then so much
As you say you did? What made you write
The Love you bore in black and white –
Drop pen – cease loving – end it all,
And give me for greeting the palm's mere touch
In place of a cheek where my kiss should fall?

Now we are sundered, is it strange
That we meet each other and say no word?
Do you think of that time when our hearts were stirred
By less than a murmur? How – once, I kept
Watch and ward o'er the long street's range
Of passionless stucco, while you slept
Somewhere, in peace, a maiden's slumber –

2

And I stood through the night, till morning's glow
Cleared the smoke from the parks below,
And you came with the dawn? How one remembers!
In my heart I have still the name and number –

*

Wherefore I place my pile on the embers.


# Overheard

So the day dragged through,
And the afternoon brought the spangles,
The sawdust smell, the tights,
The flickering, flashing lights,
The smile to acknowledge the cheer
As the rider skips and jangles
The bells. Ye gods! – 'twas queer
How the young equestriennes flew.

A programme relished, I lay
Back in my seat to gaze
On the faces around, to hear what folk say,
While the orchestra rattled and roared,
Murdering popular lays –
It was hot, too, and I felt bored.

Then a voice from behind, a rustling of dress,
The step of a man, a silence to settle,
A babble of children (how they push,
These little ones, making your coat in a mess),
A silence to settle, and after a gush
Of small talk, I sat and waited,
Shutting my eyes till the stream abated.
'Twas a tale of trouble, told in a rush.

Who was the speaker? I turned to see –
  A sharp little saucy face,
No whit abashed, gazing at me
With bead-eyes, curiously,
  With a petulant child's grimace,
As I shifted, moving her feet
    From the chair where they'd taken root,
    For the time at least; then again
I listened. Fast and fleet
    She poured out the queer little words to her friend –
    (A sort of an overgrown brute).
  I heard it out to the end –
    A story of pain.
    Here you have it, in fine
    (Her words, not mine):
    'Tried for luck in London –
                              *Voilà tout!*
    Failed, lost money, undone;
    Took to the streets for a life.
                              *Entre nous,*
    It's a terrible uphill strife,
    Like all professions – too filled.
    And now I'm in lodgings hard by,
    *Au quartième*, up in the sky.
    Visit me by and by,
They're furnished, but oh – so cold,
        So cold!'

There the queer little voice was stilled;
    She moved to a further chair
    And left me sitting there
        To think on the story told –
    Not to me, but to her friend –
Of a life that had only one end,
    And for burden, 'Oh, so cold!'

Have you ever seen on the face
    Of a child a sort of despair,
    A comical, hopeless air,
When a toy won't work, or a doll won't cry,
Or a cart runs awkwardly?

4

Well, I saw it there
　　As she moved to a further chair.
She'd broken some toy she had –
　　Or, was it a life gone bad?


## Donec Gratus Eram


HE

So long as 'twuz me alone
　　An' there wasn't no other chaps,
I was praoud as a King on 'is throne –
　　Happier tu, per'aps.


SHE

So long as 'twuz only I
　　An' there wasn't no other she
Yeou cared for so much – sure*ly*
　　I was glad as could be.


HE

But now I'm in lovv with Jane Pritt –
　　She can play the piano, she can;
An' if dyin' 'ud elp 'er a bit
　　I'd die laike a man.


SHE

Yeou'm like me. I'm in lovv with young Frye –
　　Him as lives out tu Appledore Quay;
An' if dyin' 'ud 'elp 'im I'd die –
　　Twice ovver for he.


HE

But s'posin' I threwed up Jane
　　An' niver went walkin' with she –
And come back to yeou again –
　　How 'ud that be?

Frye's sober. Yeou've allus done badly –
   An' yeou shifts like cut net-floats, yeou du:
But – I'd throw that young Frye over gladly
   An' lovv 'ee right thru!

# *Ave Imperatrix!*

*(Written on the occasion of the attempt to assassinate Queen Victoria
in March 1882)*

From every quarter of your land
   They give God thanks who turned away
Death and the needy madman's hand,
   Death-fraught, which menaced you that day.

One school of many made to make
   Men who shall hold it dearest right
To battle for their ruler's sake,
   And stake their being in the fight,

Sends greeting humble and sincere –
   Though verse be rude and poor and mean –
To you, the greatest as most dear –
   Victoria, by God's grace Our Queen!

Such greeting as should come from those
   Whose fathers faced the Sepoy hordes,
Or served you in the Russian snows,
   And, dying, left their sons their swords.

And some of us have fought for you
   Already in the Afghan pass –
Or where the scarce-seen smoke-puffs flew
   From Boer marksmen in the grass;

And all are bred to do your will
　　By land and sea – wherever flies
The Flag, to fight and follow still,
　　And work your Empire's destinies.

Once more we greet you, though unseen
　　Our greeting be, and coming slow.
Trust us, if need arise, O Queen,
　　We shall not tarry with the blow!

## *The Pious Sub's Creed*

I *do* believe in Afghan wars
　　(As far away as Peshin is)
I love to stick them in because
　　Deception most refreshin' is.
And thirteen hundred copies mean,
　　Just thirteen hundred lies you see,
And other papers think we've been
　　No end informed and wise you see.

I do believe in 'frontier news'
　　At least *cum grano salis,*
As giving scope to Wheeler's views
　　Who my eternal pal is
And anything conducive to
　　A 'scrap' with 'frontier gup' in it
Would make us most abusive to
　　All papers less well up in it.

I do believe the C.M.G.
　　The type of all perfection
And other papers mostly be
　　In need of much correction.
I do believe the native press
　　A sink of all that vicious is,

7

And each 'babu' in English dress
　　A 'darn side' too officious is.

I do believe the British Press
　　Are censors of morality
Collectively, but none the less
　　Imply their deep rascality.
I do believe commandments ten
　　To keep one should endeavour
At least, all unofficial men
　　But viceroys – hardly ever.

I do believe in Earthquake shakes
　　And tickets compliment'ry
The one at least a column makes
　　The other free-seat entry.
If any foolish Briton du'st
　　Loose captives from captivity
I do believe each journal must
　　Incontinently give it he.

I do believe in tiger skins
　　From fourteen feet to twenty
At least when for my many sins
　　Mail items aren't in plenty.
I do believe in 'monster' leaps
　　By 'liliputian' horses
And dig out 'flying shots' in heaps
　　From 'most authentic sources'.

I do believe the scissors are
　　The world's most sure foundation
And pasting paragraphs by far
　　The finest occupation.
I do believe that naught too low
　　Or high for daily grist is –
*I think the Bible's true – I know*
　　*The Indian Civil List is.*

# A Vision of India

Mother India, wan and thin,
    Here is forage come your way;
Take the young Civilian in,
    Kill him swiftly as you may.

Smite him with the deadly breath
    From your crowded cities sped;
Still the heart that beats beneath
    That girl's picture o'er his bed.

Brains that thought and lips that kissed,
    Mouldering under alien clay,
Stir a stagnant Civil List,
    Help us on our upward way.

(Ice the amber whisky-peg!
    Every man that yields to thee
Gives his juniors each a leg,
    Shakes the sere Pagoda-Tree.)

Well indeed we know your power,
    Goddess of our deep devotion,
Who can grant us in an hour
    Steps of rapidest promotion.

Lurking in our daily grub,
    Where the untinned *degchies* lie;
Smiting gaily at the Club,
    O'er the card-room's revelry.

Chaperon to many a maid,
    Calling, when the music dies,
To a stiller, deeper shade
    Than the dim-lit balconies.

(Fill the long-necked glass with whisky!
　　Every man that owns thy sway
Leaves a widow, mostly frisky,
　　Makes the gossip of a day.)

Brown and Jones and Smith shall die;
　　We succeed to all their places,
Bear the badge of slavery,
　　Sunken eyes and pallid faces.

Laughter that is worse than tears
　　Is our portion in the land,
And the tombstones of our peers
　　Make the steps whereon we stand.


# The Flight of the Bucket


*Pre-admonisheth* THE WRITER:
H'm, for a subject it is well enough!
Who wrote 'Sordello' finds no subject tough.

Well, Jack and Jill – God knows the life they led
(The poet never told us, more's the pity)
Pent up in some damp kennel of their own,
Beneath the hillside; but it once befell
That Jack or Jill, niece, cousin, uncle, aunt
(Some one of all the brood) would wash or scour –
Rinse out a cess-pit, swab the kennel floor,
And water (*liquor vitae*, Lawson calls,
But I – I hold by whisky. Never mind;
I didn't mean to hurt your feelings, sir,
And missed the scrap o' blue at buttonhole –)
Spring water was the needful at the time,
So they must climb the hill for't. Well and good.
We all climb hills, I take it, on some quest,
Maybe for less than stinking (I forgot!

10

I mean than wholesome) water ... Ferret out
The rotten bucket from the lumber-shed,
Weave ropes and splice the handle – off they go
To where the cold spring bubbles up i' the cleft,
And sink the bucket brimful in the spate.
Then downwards – hanging back? (You bet your life
The girl's share fell upon Jack's shoulders.) Down,
Down to the bottom – all but – trip, slip, squelch!
And guggle-guggle goes the bucketful
Back to the earth, and Jack's a broken head,
And swears amid the heather does our Jack.
(A man would swear who watched both blood and bucket,
One dripping down his forehead, t'other fled,
*Clinkety-tinkle*, to the stones below,
A good half-hour's trudge to get it back.)
Jack, therefore, as I said, exploded straight
In brimstone-flavoured language. You, of course,
Maintain he bore it calmly – not a bit.
A good bucolic curse that rent the cliffs
And frightened for a moment quaking Jill
Out of the limp, unmeaning girl's tee-hee
That womankind delight in ... Here we end
The first verse – there's a deal to study in't.

*

So much for Jack – but there's a Fate above,
A cosmic force that blunders into right,
Just when the strained sense hints at revolution
Because the world's great fly-wheel runs aslant –
And up go Jill's red kibes. (You think I'm wrong;
And Fate was napping at the time; perhaps
You're right.) We'll call it Devil's agency
That sent the shrieking sister on her head,
And knocked the tangled locks against the stones.
Well, down went Jill, but wasn't hurt. Oh, no!
The Devil pads the world to suit his own,
And packs the cards according. Down went Jill
Unhurt. And Jack trots off to bed, poor brute,
Fist welted into eyeball, mouth agape
For yelling – your bucolic always yells –

And out of his domestic pharmacy
Rips forth the cruet-stand, upsets the cat,
And ravages the store-room for his balm.
*Eureka*! – but he didn't use that word –
A pound of candles, corpse-like, side by side,
Wrapped up in his medicament. Out, knife!
Cut string, and strip the shrouding from the lot!
Steep swift and jam it on the gaping cut;
Then bedward – cursing man and fiends alike.

*

Now back to Jill. She wasn't hurt, I said,
And all the woman's spite was up in arms.
So Jack's abed. She slips, peeks through the door,
And sees the split head like a luggage-label,
Halved, quartered, on the pillow. 'Ee-ki-ree,
Tee-hee-hee-hee,' she giggles through the crack,
Much as the Roman ladies grinned – don't smile –
To see the dabbled bodies in the sand
Appealing to their benches for a sign.
Down thumbs, and giggle louder – so did Jill.
But mark now! Comes the mother round the door,
Red-hot from climbing up the hill herself,
And caught the graceless giggler. Whack! flack! whack!
Here's Nemesis whichever way you like!
*She* didn't stop to argue. Given a head
Broken, a woman chuckling at the door,
And here's your circumstantial evidence complete.
Whack! while Jack sniffs and sniggers from the bed.
I like that horny-handed mother o' Jill.
The world's best women died, sir, long ago.
Well, Jack's avenged; as for the other, *gr-r-r-r*!

12

# Jane Smith

I journeyed, on a winter's day,
   Across the lonely wold;
No bird did sing upon the spray,
   And it was very cold.

I had a coach with horses four,
   Three white (though one was black),
And on they went the common o'er,
   Nor swiftness did they lack.

A little girl ran by the side,
   And she was pinched and thin.
'Oh, please, sir, *do* give me a ride!
   I'm fetching mother's gin.'

'Enter my coach, sweet child,' said I;
   'For you shall ride with me,
And I will get you your supply
   Of mother's eau-de-vie.'

The publican was stern and cold,
   And said: 'Her mother's score
Is writ, as you shall soon behold,
   Behind the bar-room door!'

I blotted out the score with tears,
   And paid the money down,
And took the maid of thirteen years
   Back to her mother's town;

And though the past with surges wild
   Fond memories may sever,
The vision of that happy child
   Will leave my spirit never!

# The Vision of Hamid Ali

This came to him by night – the *ganja* burnt
To powder, and the City sunk in sleep.

Azizun of the Dauri Bagh; the Pearl;
And Hamid Ali of the Delhi Gate
Were present, when the Muezzin called to prayer
At midnight from the Mosque of Wuzeer Khan,
Drinking the *ganja*, drowsy with its fumes
Above the dying *chillam*. I, the Scribe,
Was with them and the words I write are true;
(Albeit Hamid spoke against the Twelve,
And Islam and the Prophet. God is judge
Whether the *ganja* moved him or his soul.)
Azizun's anklets tinkled when she turned
In slumber; and the Pearl of Courtezans
Laughed softly at some fancy of her brain,
Born of the *ganja*. Hamid Ali lay
As dead upon the cushions by the door
For half a watch; and then he cried to me: –
'The thing is hopeless and an idle dream!
I saw it even now. O Moulvie! write!'
(Before the Perfect Flower had dulled our brains,
Azizun; Hamid Ali; I; the Pearl,
Spoke of the Prophet and the other, Christ
Our rulers worship; and men's minds in Roum;
And whether Islam shall arise again
And drive the Christ across the Western sea
As people hold shall be in two more years,
When from the North the Armies of the North
Pour like the Indus and our rulers fly,
And Islam and the Sword make all things clean.)
    I wrote – my brain was heavy with the drug: –
'The Mosque has fallen. Hamid Ali saw
The *khashi* on the gateways peel and flake;
The domes sink inwards and the minarets
Break at the base and crumble like the dust
The wind uplifts in Sind and leaves again

No bigger than an ant-hill. It has fallen.
I, Hamid, saw and knew the meaning. Turn,
Turn ye to slumber. Fold your hands and sleep.
Ours was an idle dream.' The Pearl laughed low: –
'I dreamt no dream but ye. My breasts are real;
My lips; my love, O Hamid! Nothing else,
Nor Islam nor the Prophet nor the Twelve.
Turn ye to slumber. Fold your hands and sleep.'
      And Hamid answered: – 'Fold your hands and sleep
Not yet till ye have heard the vision. Write!'
(I wrote and marvelled, as the Muezzin called.)
'Nor Islam, nor the Prophet, nor the Twelve,
Nor Christ, nor Buddha, nor the other gods
Avail us. Lo! The Mosque fell into dust;
And with it fell the Prophet and the Twelve;
The Banner and the Crescent rang below,
And with them fell the Cross, the Wheel, the Flowers;
Parvati broken at the waist, and He,
The calm-eyed Buddha, handless, crushed and maimed.
The Priests with these. I, Hamid, saw them fall
And knew our dream was hopeless. Never more
The Banner or the Cross will lift themselves.
(Write, Moulvie.) Underneath the Seven Stars,
Blood red and golden, to the dark plain's verge
There swept the sharp edge of a monstrous sword
That lit the firmament as does the sun;
And blood was falling from the haft and point;
And where it fell the Mosques of all the lands
Fell also, burnt with fire; and the Priests
Cried to the Heavens that their gods were dead,
And none remained to feed their ministers
Or tend the altars; and the great sword fell
Above Mahomet and the other men,
And broke into ten thousand drops of blood
Before it faded and I woke to you,
Azizun and the Pearl. I, Hamid, saw
And read the meaning of the vision!'
                                        Soft
The anklets tinkled as Azizun woke.
Then Hamid hollow-eyed rose from the couch
And staggered doorward – but the Pearl withstood

15

And only laughed: – 'Oh, Hamid, will you take
Me for your Prophet if I read the dream?'
And Hamid answered: – 'Surely. It is writ' –
Whereat the Pearl laughed louder: – 'Is it writ?
Who wrote, and wherefore? Let the vision go,
For I at least am real.'
     Then the dawn …
Swept like a sea into the gully. I,
Still heavy with the *ganja*, held my peace
And marvelled that a man should so blaspheme …
God grant it was the *ganja*. Otherwise
Hamid is lost for ever, with the Pearl.


## *Of Birthdays*


For us Life's wheel runs backward. Other nests
  Are stripped of all their fledglings when our Fate
  Pitying may be, a childhood desolate,
Brings home deferred – unparted each one rests
  Beneath one roof.
     But the year's fitful span
  Brings change & growth & half displeased you say
  Musing upon the babes of yesterday:
'Behold, she is a woman; He a man.'
Yet, spite of all, the childish wonder clings
  About our spirits when we hear him say –
  Our Father – 'Children I was born to-day.'
And we return to nursery wonderings
  Back comes the childish question to the tongue
  Father a child! – Was Father ever young?

# The Story of Uriah

*('Now there were two men in one city; the one rich, and the other poor.')*

Jack Barrett went to Quetta
    Because they told him to.
He left his wife at Simla
    On three-fourths his monthly screw.
Jack Barrett died at Quetta
    Ere the next month's pay he drew.

Jack Barrett went to Quetta.
    He didn't understand
The reason of his transfer
    From the pleasant mountain-land.
The season was September,
    And it killed him out of hand.

Jack Barrett went to Quetta
    And there gave up the ghost,
Attempting two men's duty
    In that very healthy post;
And Mrs. Barrett mourned for him
    Five lively months at most.

Jack Barrett's bones at Quetta
    Enjoy profound repose;
But I shouldn't be astonished
    If *now* his spirit knows
The reason for his transfer
    From the Himalayan snows.

And, when the Last Great Bugle Call
    Adown the Hurnai throbs,
And the last grim joke is entered
    In the big black Book of Jobs,
And Quetta graveyards give again
    Their victims to the air,
I shouldn't like to be the man
    Who sent Jack Barrett there.

# A Code of Morals

*Lest you should think this story true*
*I merely mention I*
*Evolved it lately. 'Tis a most*
*Unmitigated misstatement.*


Now Jones had left his new-wed bride to keep his house in order,
And hied away to the Hurrum Hills above the Afghan border,
To sit on a rock with a heliograph; but ere he left he taught
His wife the working of the Code that sets the miles at naught.

And Love had made him very sage, as Nature made her fair;
So Cupid and Apollo linked, *per* heliograph, the pair.
At dawn, across the Hurrum Hills, he flashed her counsel wise –
At e'en, the dying sunset bore her husband's homilies.

He warned her 'gainst seductive youths in scarlet clad and gold,
As much as 'gainst the blandishments paternal of the old;
But kept his gravest warnings for (hereby the ditty hangs)
That snowy-haired Lothario, Lieutenant-General Bangs.

'Twas General Bangs, with Aide and Staff, who tittupped on the
                                                            way,
When they beheld a heliograph tempestuously at play.
They thought of Border risings, and of stations sacked and burnt –
So stopped to take the message down – and this is what they
                                                          learnt –

'Dash dot dot, dot, dot dash, dot dash dot' twice. The General
                                                            swore.
Was ever General Officer addressed as 'dear' before?
'My Love', i' faith! 'My Duck', Gadzooks! 'My darling
                                                    popsy-wop!'
'Spirit of great Lord Wolseley, *who* is on that mountain-top?'

The artless Aide-de-camp was mute, the gilded Staff were still,
As, dumb with pent-up mirth, they booked that message from
the hill;
For clear as summer lightning-flare, the husband's warning ran: –
'Don't dance or ride with General Bangs – a most immoral man.'

(At dawn, across the Hurrum Hills, he flashed her counsel wise –
But, howsoever Love be blind, the world at large hath eyes.)
With damnatory dot and dash he heliographed his wife
Some interesting details of the General's private life.

The artless Aide-de-camp was mute, the shining Staff were still,
And red and ever redder grew the General's shaven gill.
And this is what he said at last (his feelings matter not): –
'I think we've tapped a private line. Hi! Threes about there! Trot!'

All honour unto Bangs, for ne'er did Jones thereafter know
By word or act official who read off that helio.
But the tale is on the Frontier, and from Michni to Mooltan
They know the worthy General as 'that most immoral man'.

## The Man Who Could Write

*Shun – shun the Bowl! That fatal, facile drink*
*Has ruined many geese who dipped their quills in't;*
*Bribe, murder, marry, but steer clear of Ink*
*Save when you write receipts for paid-up bills in't.*
*There may be silver in the 'blue-black' – all*
*I know of is the iron and the gall.*


Boanerges Blitzen, servant of the Queen,
Is a dismal failure – is a Might-have-been.
In a luckless moment he discovered men
Rise to high position through a ready pen.

Boanerges Blitzen argued therefore – 'I,
With the selfsame weapon, can attain as high.'
Only he did not possess when he made the trial,
Wicked wit of Colvin, irony of Lyall.

(Men who spar with Government need, to back their blows,
Something more than ordinary journalistic prose.)

Never young Civilian's prospects were so bright,
Till an Indian paper found that he could write:
Never young Civilian's prospects were so dark,
When the wretched Blitzen wrote to make his mark.

Certainly he scored it, bold, and black, and firm,
In that Indian paper – made his seniors squirm,
Quoted office scandals, wrote the tactless truth –
Was there ever known a more misguided youth?

When the Rag he wrote for praised his plucky game,
Boanerges Blitzen felt that this was Fame;
When the men he wrote of shook their heads and swore,
Boanerges Blitzen only wrote the more:

Posed as Young Ithuriel, resolute and grim,
Till he found promotion didn't come to him;
Till he found that reprimands weekly were his lot,
And his many Districts curiously hot.

Till he found his furlough strangely hard to win,
Boanerges Blitzen didn't care a pin:
Then it seemed to dawn on him something wasn't right –
Boanerges Blitzen put it down to 'spite';

Languished in a District desolate and dry;
Watched the Local Government yearly pass him by;
Wondered where the hitch was; called it most unfair.

\*

That was seven years ago – and he still is there!

# My Rival

I go to concert, party, ball –
  What profit is in these?
I sit alone against the wall
  And strive to look at ease.
The incense that is mine by right
  They burn before Her shrine;
And that's because I'm seventeen
  And She is forty-nine.

I cannot check my girlish blush,
  My colour comes and goes.
I redden to my finger-tips,
  And sometimes to my nose.
But She is white where white should be,
  And red where red should shine.
The blush that flies at seventeen
  Is fixed at forty-nine.

I wish *I* had Her constant cheek;
  I wish that I could sing
All sorts of funny little songs,
  Not quite the proper thing.
I'm very *gauche* and very shy,
  Her jokes aren't in my line;
And, worst of all, I'm seventeen
  While She is forty-nine.

The young men come, the young men go,
  Each pink and white and neat,
She's older than their mothers, but
  They grovel at Her feet.
They walk beside Her 'rickshaw wheels –
  None ever walk by mine;
And that's because I'm seventeen
  And She is forty-nine.

She rides with half a dozen men,
    (She calls them 'boys' and 'mashes'),
I trot along the Mall alone;
    My prettiest frocks and sashes
Don't help to fill my programme-card,
    And vainly I repine
From ten to two A.M. Ah me!
    Would I were forty-nine!

She calls me 'darling', 'pet', and 'dear',
    And 'sweet retiring maid'.
I'm always at the back, I know –
    She puts me in the shade.
She introduces me to men –
    'Cast' lovers, I opine,
For sixty takes to seventeen,
    Nineteen to forty-nine.

But even She must older grow
    And end Her dancing days,
She can't go on for ever so
    At concerts, balls, and plays.
One ray of priceless hope I see
    Before my footsteps shine;
Just think, that She'll be eighty-one
    When I am forty-nine!

# La Nuit Blanche

*A much-discerning Public hold*
*The Singer generally sings*
*Of personal and private things,*
*And prints and sells his past for gold.*

*Whatever I may here disclaim,*
*The very clever folk I sing to*
*Will most indubitably cling to*
*Their pet delusion, just the same.*

I had seen, as dawn was breaking
    And I staggered to my rest,
Tara Devi softly shaking
    From the Cart Road to the crest.
I had seen the spurs of Jakko
    Heave and quiver, swell and sink.
Was it Earthquake or tobacco,
    Day of Doom or Night of Drink?

In the full, fresh fragrant morning
    I observed a camel crawl,
Laws of gravitation scorning,
    On the ceiling and the wall.
Then I watched a fender walking,
    And I heard grey leeches sing,
And a red-hot monkey talking
    Did not seem the proper thing.

Then a Creature, skinned and crimson,
    Ran about the floor and cried,
And they said that I had the 'jims' on,
    And they dosed me with bromide,
And they locked me in my bedroom –
    Me and one wee Blood-Red Mouse –
Though I said: – 'To give my head room
    You had best unroof the house.'

23

But my words were all unheeded,
   Though I told the grave M.D.
That the treatment really needed
   Was a dip in open sea
That was lapping just below me,
   Smooth as silver, white as snow –
And it took three men to throw me
   When I found I could not go.

Half the night I watched the Heavens
   Fizz like '81 champagne –
Fly to sixes and to sevens,
   Wheel and thunder back again;
And when all was peace and order
   Save one planet nailed askew,
Much I wept because my warder
   Would not let me set it true.

After frenzied hours of waiting,
   When the Earth and Skies were dumb,
Pealed an awful voice dictating
   An interminable sum,
Changing to a tangled story –
   'What she said you said I said' –
Till the Moon arose in glory,
   And I found her ... in my head;

Then a Face came, blind and weeping,
   And It couldn't wipe its eyes,
And It muttered I was keeping
   Back the moonlight from the skies;
So I patted it for pity,
   But it whistled shrill with wrath,
And a huge, black Devil City
   Poured its peoples on my path.

So I fled with steps uncertain
    On a thousand-year long race,
But the bellying of the curtain
    Kept me always in one place;
While the tumult rose and maddened
    To the roar of Earth on fire,
Ere it ebbed and sank and saddened
    To a whisper tense as wire.

In intolerable stillness
    Rose one little, little star,
And it chuckled at my illness,
    And it mocked me from afar;
And its brethren came and eyed me,
    Called the Universe to aid,
Till I lay, with naught to hide me,
    'Neath the Scorn of All Things Made.

Dun and saffron, robed and splendid,
    Broke the solemn, pitying Day,
And I knew my pains were ended,
    And I turned and tried to pray;
But my speech was shattered wholly,
    And I wept as children weep.
Till the dawn-wind, softly, slowly,
    Brought to burning eyelids sleep.


## Arithmetic on the Frontier


A great and glorious thing it is
    To learn, for seven years or so,
The Lord knows what of that and this,
    Ere reckoned fit to face the foe –
The flying bullet down the Pass,
That whistles clear: 'All flesh is grass.'

Three hundred pounds per annum spent
    On making brain and body meeter
For all the murderous intent
    Comprised in 'villainous saltpetre'!
And after? – ask the Yusufzaies
What comes of all our 'ologies.

A scrimmage in a Border Station –
    A canter down some dark defile –
Two thousand pounds of education
    Drops to a ten-rupee *jezail* –
The Crammer's boast, the Squadron's pride,
Shot like a rabbit in a ride!

No proposition Euclid wrote,
    No formulae the text-books know,
Will turn the bullet from your coat,
    Or ward the tulwar's downward blow
Strike hard who cares – shoot straight who can –
The odds are on the cheaper man.

One sword-knot stolen from the camp
    Will pay for all the school expenses
Of any Kurrum Valley scamp
    Who knows no word of moods and tenses,
But, being blessed with perfect sight,
Picks off our messmates left and right.

With home-bred hordes the hillsides teem,
    The troopships bring us one by one,
At vast expense of time and steam,
    To slay Afridis where they run.
The 'captives of our bow and spear'
Are cheap, alas! as we are dear.

# One Viceroy Resigns

Lord Dufferin to Lord Lansdowne: –

So here's your Empire. No more wine, then? Good.
We'll clear the Aides and *khitmutgars* away.
(You'll know that fat old fellow with the knife –
He keeps the Name Book, talks in English, too,
And almost thinks himself the Government.)
O Youth, Youth, Youth! Forgive me, you're so young.
Forty from sixty – twenty years of work
And power to back the working. *Ay de mi!*
You want to know, you want to see, to touch
And, by your lights, to act. It's natural.
I wonder can I help you? Let me try.
You saw – what did you see from Bombay east?
Enough to frighten any one but me?
Neat that! It frightened Me in Eighty-Four!
You shouldn't take a man from Canada
And bid him smoke in powder-magazines;
Nor with a Reputation such as – Bah!
That ghost has haunted me for twenty years,
My Reputation now full-blown. Your fault!
Yours, with your stories of the strife at Home,
Who's up, who's down, who leads and who is led –
One reads so much, one hears so little here.
Well, now's your turn of exile. I go back
To Rome and leisure. All roads lead to Rome,
Or books – the refuge of the destitute.
When you ... that brings me back to India. See!
    Start clear. I couldn't. Egypt served my turn.
You'll never plumb the Oriental mind,
And if you did, it isn't worth the toil.
Think of a sleek French priest in Canada;
Divide by twenty half-breeds. Multiply
By twice the Sphinx's silence. There's your East,
And you're as wise as ever. So am I.
    Accept on trust and work in darkness, strike
At venture, stumble forward, make your mark,

(It's chalk on granite), then thank God no flame
Leaps from the rock to shrivel mark and man.
I'm clear – my mark is made. Three months of drought
Had ruined much. It rained and washed away
The specks that might have gathered on my Name.
I took a country twice the size of France,
And shuttered up one doorway in the North.
I stand by those. You'll find that both will pay,
I pledged my Name on both – they're yours to-night.
Hold to them – they hold fame enough for two.
I'm old, but I shall live till Burma pays.
Men there – *not* German traders – Crosthwaite knows –
You'll find it in my papers. For the North
Guns always – quietly – but always guns.
You've seen your Council? Yes, they'll try to rule,
And prize their Reputations. Have you met
A grim lay-reader with a taste for coins,
And faith in Sin most men withhold from God?
He's gone to England. Ripon knew his grip
And kicked. A Council always has its Hopes.
They look for nothing from the West but Death
Or Bath or Bournemouth. Here's their ground.
                                             They fight
Until the Middle Classes take them back,
One of ten millions plus a C.S.I.,
Or drop in harness. Legion of the Lost?
Not altogether. Earnest, narrow men,
But chiefly earnest, and they'll do your work,
And end by writing letters to the *Times*.
(Shall I write letters, answering Hunter – fawn
With Ripon on the Yorkshire grocers? Ugh!)
They have their Reputations. Look to one –
I work with him – the smallest of them all,
White-haired, red-faced, who sat the plunging horse
Out in the garden. He's your right-hand man,
And dreams of tilting Wolseley from the throne,
But while he dreams gives work we cannot buy;
He has his Reputation – wants the Lords
By way of Frontier Roads. Meantime, I think,
He values very much the hand that falls
Upon his shoulder at the Council table –

Hates cats and knows his business. *Which is yours.*
Your business! Twice a hundred million souls.
Your business! I could tell you what I did
Some nights of Eighty-five, at Simla, worth
A Kingdom's ransom. When a big ship drives
God knows to what new reef, the man at the wheel
Prays with the passengers. They lose their lives,
Or rescued go their way; but he's no man
To take his trick at the wheel again. That's worse
Than drowning. Well, a galled Mashobra mule
(You'll see Mashobra) passed me on the Mall,
And I was – some fool's wife had ducked and bowed
To show the others I would stop and speak.
Then the mule fell – three galls, a hand-breadth each,
Behind the withers. Mrs Whatsisname
Leers at the mule and me by turns, thweet thoul!
'How could they make him carry such a load!'
I saw – it isn't often I dream dreams –
More than the mule that minute – smoke and flame
From Simla to the haze below. That's weak.
You're younger. You'll dream dreams before you've done.
You've youth, that's one;  good workmen – that means two
Fair chances in your favour. Fate's the third.
I know what *I* did. Do you ask me, 'Preach?'
I answer by my past or else go back
To platitudes of rule – or take you thus
In confidence and say: – 'You know the trick:
You've governed Canada. You know. *You* know!'
And all the while commend you to Fate's hand
(Here at the top one loses sight o' God),
Commend you, then, to something more than you –
The Other People's blunders and … that's all.
I'd agonise to serve you if I could.
It's incommunicable, like the cast
That drops the hackle with the gut adry.
Too much – too little – there's your salmon lost!
And so I tell you nothing –wish you luck,
And wonder – how I wonder! – for your sake!
And triumph for my own. You're young, you're young,
You hold to half a hundred Shibboleths.
I'm old. I followed Power to the last,

Gave her my best, and Power followed Me.
It's worth it – on my soul I'm speaking plain,
Here by the claret glasses! – worth it all.
I gave – no matter what I gave – I win.
I *know* I win. Mine's work, good work that lives!
A country twice the size of France – the North
Safeguarded. That's my record: sink the rest
And better if you can. The Rains may serve,
Rupees may rise – threepence will give you Fame –
It's rash to hope for sixpence. If they rise
Get guns, more guns, and lift the salt-tax ... Oh!
I told you what the Congress meant or thought?
I'll answer nothing. Half a year will prove
The full extent of time and thought you'll spare
To Congress. Ask a Lady Doctor *once*
How little Begums see the light – deduce
Thence how the True Reformer's child is born.
It's interesting, curious ... and vile.
I told the Turk he was a gentleman.
I told the Russian that his Tartar veins
Bled pure Parisian ichor; and he purred.
The Congress doesn't purr. I think it swears.
You're young – you'll swear too ere you've reached the end.
The End! God help you, if there be a God.
(There must be one to startle Gladstone's soul
In that new land where all the wires are cut,
And Cross snores anthems on the asphodel.)
God help you! And I'd help you if I could,
But that's beyond me. Yes, your speech was crude.
Sound claret after olives – yours and mine;
But Médoc slips into vin ordinaire.
(I'll drink my first at Genoa to your health.)
Raise it to Hock. You'll never catch my style.
And, after all, the middle-classes grip
The middle-class – for Brompton talk Earl's Court.
Perhaps you're right. I'll see you in the *Times* –
A quarter-column of eye-searing print,
A leader once a quarter – then a war;
The Strand a-bellow through the fog: – 'Defeat!'
''Orrible slaughter!' While you lie awake
And wonder. Oh, you'll wonder ere you're free!

I wonder now. The four years slide away
So fast, so fast, and leave me here alone.
Reay, Colvin, Lyall, Roberts, Buck, the rest,
Princes and Powers of Darkness, troops and trains,
(I *cannot* sleep in trains), land piled on land,
Whitewash and weariness, red rockets, dust,
White snows that mocked me, palaces – with draughts,
And Westland with the drafts he couldn't pay,
Poor Wilson reading his obituary
Before he died, and Hope, the man with bones,
And Aitchison a dripping mackintosh
At Council in the Rains, his grating 'Sirrr'
Half drowned by Hunter's silky: 'Bât my lahd.'
Hunterian always: Marshal spinning plates
Or standing on his head; the Rent Bill's roar,
A hundred thousand speeches, much red cloth,
And Smiths thrice happy if I called them Jones,
(I can't remember half their names) or reined
My pony on the Mall to greet their wives.
More trains, more troops, more dust, and then all's done.
Four years, and I forget. If I forget,
How will *they* bear me in their minds? The North
Safeguarded – nearly (Roberts knows the rest),
A country twice the size of France annexed.
That stays at least. The rest may pass – may pass –
Your heritage – and I can teach you naught.
'High trust', 'vast honour', 'interests twice as vast',
'Due reverence to your Council' – keep to those.
I envy you the twenty years you've gained,
But not the five to follow. What's that? One!
Two! – Surely not so late. Good-night. *Don't* dream.

# The Winners

*(The Story of the Gadsbys)*

What is the moral? Who rides may read.
When the night is thick and the tracks are blind
A friend at a pinch is a friend indeed,
But a fool to wait for the laggard behind.
Down to Gehenna or up to the Throne,
He travels the fastest who travels alone.

White hands cling to the tightened rein,
Slipping the spur from the booted heel,
Tenderest voices cry 'Turn again!'
Red lips tarnish the scabbarded steel.
High hopes faint on a warm hearth-stone –
He travels the fastest who travels alone.

One may fall but he falls by himself –
Falls by himself with himself to blame.
One may attain and to him is pelf –
Loot of the city in Gold or Fame.
Plunder of earth shall be all his own
Who travels the fastest and travels alone.

Wherefore the more ye be helpen and stayed,
Stayed by a friend in the hour of toil,
Sing the heretical song I have made –
His be the labour and yours be the spoil.
Win by his aid and the aid disown –
He travels the fastest who travels alone!

# The Love Song of Har Dyal

*('Beyond the Pale'– Plain Tales from the Hills)*

Alone upon the housetops to the North
I turn and watch the lightnings in the sky –
The glamour of thy footsteps in the North.
*Come back to me, Beloved, or I die!*

Below my feet the still bazaar is laid –
Far, far below the weary camels lie –
The camels and the captives of thy raid.
*Come back to me, Beloved, or I die!*

My father's wife is old and harsh with years,
And drudge of all my father's house am I –
My bread is sorrow and my drink is tears.
*Come back to me, Beloved, or I die!*

# Inscription in Copy of Plain Tales from the Hills Presented to Mrs Hill

Between the gum pot and the shears,
    The weapons of my grimy trade,
In divers moods and various years
    These forty foolish yarns were made.

And some were writ to fill a page
    And some – but these are not so many –
To soothe a finely moral rage
    And all to turn an honest penny.

And some I gathered from my friends
    And some I looted from my foes,
And some – All's fish that Heaven sends –
    Are histories of private woes.

And some are Truth, and some are Lie,
    And some exactly half and half,
I've heard some made a woman cry –
    I *know* some made a woman laugh.

I do not view them with delight
    And, since I know that you may read 'em,
I'd like to thoroughly rewrite,
    Remould, rebuild, retouch, reword 'em.

Would they were worthier. That's too late –
    Cracked pictures stand no further stippling.
Forgive the faults.

*March '88*

To Mrs Hill
    From Rudyard Kipling.


## The Ballad of East and West
### 1889

*Oh, East is East, and West is West, and never the twain shall meet,*
*Till Earth and Sky stand presently at God's great Judgment Seat;*
*But there is neither East nor West, Border, nor Breed, nor Birth,*
*When two strong men stand face to face, though they come from the*
                              *ends of the earth!*

Kamal is out with twenty men to raise the Border-side,
And he has lifted the Colonel's mare that is the Colonel's pride.
He has lifted her out of the stable-door between the dawn and
                            the day,

And turned the calkins upon her feet, and ridden her far away.
Then up and spoke the Colonel's son that led a troop of the Guides:
'Is there never a man of all my men can say where Kamal hides?'
Then up and spoke Mohammed Khan, the son of the Ressaldar:
'If ye know the track of the morning-mist, ye know where his
pickets are.
At dusk he harries the Abazai – at dawn he is into Bonair,
But he must go by Fort Bukloh to his own place to fare,
So if ye gallop to Fort Bukloh as fast as a bird can fly,
By the favour of God ye may cut him off ere he win to the
Tongue of Jagai.
But if he be past the Tongue of Jagai, right swiftly turn ye then,
For the length and the breadth of that grisly plain is sown with
Kamal's men.
There is rock to the left, and rock to the right, and low lean thorn
between,
And ye may hear a breech-bolt snick where never a man is seen.'
The Colonel's son has taken a horse, and a raw rough dun was he,
With the mouth of a bell and the heart of Hell and the head of a
gallows-tree.
The Colonel's son to the Fort has won, they bid him stay to eat –
Who rides at the tail of a Border thief, he sits not long at his meat.
He's up and away from Fort Bukloh as fast as he can fly,
Till he was aware of his father's mare in the gut of the Tongue of
Jagai,
Till he was aware of his father's mare with Kamal upon her back,
And when he could spy the white of her eye, he made the pistol
crack.
He has fired once, he has fired twice, but the whistling ball went
wide.
'Ye shoot like a soldier,' Kamal said. 'Show now if ye can ride!'
It's up and over the Tongue of Jagai, as blown dust-devils go,
The dun he fled like a stag of ten, but the mare like a barren doe.
The dun he leaned against the bit and slugged his head above,
But the red mare played with the snaffle-bars, as a maiden plays
with a glove.
There was rock to the left and rock to the right, and low lean
thorn between,
And thrice he heard a breech-bolt snick tho' never a man was seen.
They have ridden the low moon out of the sky, their hoofs drum
up the dawn,

The dun he went like a wounded bull, but the mare like a
                                        new-roused fawn.
The dun he fell at a water-course – in a woeful heap fell he,
And Kamal has turned the red mare back, and pulled the rider
                                                    free.
He has knocked the pistol out of his hand – small room was
                                                there to strive,
"'Twas only by favour of mine,' quoth he, 'ye rode so long alive:
There was not a rock for twenty mile, there was not a clump of
                                                    tree,
But covered a man of my own men with his rifle cocked on his
                                                    knee.
If I had raised my bridle-hand, as I have held it low,
The little jackals that flee so fast were feasting all in a row:
If I had bowed my head on my breast, as I have held it high,
The kite that whistles above us now were gorged till she could
                                                    not fly.'
Lightly answered the Colonel's son: 'Do good to bird and beast,
But count who come for the broken meats before thou makest a
                                                    feast.
If there should follow a thousand swords to carry my bones away,
Belike the price of a jackal's meal were more than a thief could pay.
They will feed their horse on the standing crop, their men on the
                                                garnered grain,
The thatch of the byres will serve their fires when all the cattle
                                                are slain.
But if thou thinkest the price be fair – thy brethren wait to sup,
The hound is kin to the jackal-spawn – howl, dog, and call them
                                                    up!
And if thou thinkest the price be high, in steer and gear and stack,
Give me my father's mare again, and I'll fight my own way back!'
Kamal has gripped him by the hand and set him upon his feet.
'No talk shall be of dogs,' said he, 'when wolf and grey wolf meet.
May I eat dirt if thou hast hurt of me in deed or breath;
What dam of lances brought thee forth to jest at the dawn with
                                                    Death?'
Lightly answered the Colonel's son: 'I hold by the blood of my clan:
Take up the mare for my father's gift – by God, she has carried a
                                                    man!'
The red mare ran to the Colonel's son, and nuzzled against his
                                                    breast;

36

'We be two strong men,' said Kamal then, 'but she loveth the
                                                younger best.
So she shall go with a lifter's dower, my turquoise-studded rein,
My 'broidered saddle and saddle-cloth, and silver stirrups twain.'
The Colonel's son a pistol drew, and held it muzzle-end,
'Ye have taken the one from a foe,' said he. 'Will ye take the
                                        mate from a friend?'
'A gift for a gift,' said Kamal straight; 'a limb for the risk of a limb.
Thy father has sent his son to me, I'll send my son to him!'
With that he whistled his only son, that dropped from a
                                        mountain-crest –
He trod the ling like a buck in spring, and he looked like a lance
                                                in rest.
'Now here is thy master,' Kamal said, 'who leads a troop of the
                                                Guides,
And thou must ride at his left side as shield on shoulder rides.
Till Death or I cut loose the tie, at camp and board and bed,
Thy life is his – thy fate it is to guard him with thy head.
So, thou must eat the White Queen's meat, and all her foes are
                                                thine,
And thou must harry thy father's hold for the peace of the
                                                Border-line,
And thou must make a trooper tough and hack thy way to
                                                power –
Belike they will raise thee to Ressaldar when I am hanged in
                                        Peshawur!'


They have looked each other between the eyes, and there they
                                        found no fault,
They have taken the Oath of the Brother-in-Blood on leavened
                                        bread and salt:
They have taken the Oath of the Brother-in-Blood on fire and
                                        fresh-cut sod,
On the hilt and the haft of the Khyber knife, and the Wondrous
                                        Names of God.


The Colonel's son he rides the mare and Kamal's boy the dun,
And two have come back to Fort Bukloh where there went forth
                                                but one.
And when they drew to the Quarter-Guard, full twenty swords
                                                flew clear –

There was not a man but carried his feud with the blood of the
                                                        mountaineer.
'Ha' done! ha' done!' said the Colonel's son. 'Put up the steel at
                                                        your sides!
Last night ye had struck at a Border thief – to-night 'tis a man of
                                                        the Guides!'

*Oh, East is East, and West is West, and never the twain shall meet,*
*Till Earth and Sky stand presently at God's great Judgment Seat;*
*But there is neither East nor West, Border, nor Breed, nor Birth,*
*When two strong men stand face to face, though they come from the*
                                                        *ends of the earth!*

## The Conundrum of the Workshops
### 1890

When the flush of a new-born sun fell first on Eden's green and
                                                        gold,
Our father Adam sat under the Tree and scratched with a stick
                                                        in the mould;
And the first rude sketch that the world had seen was joy to his
                                                        mighty heart,
Till the Devil whispered behind the leaves, 'It's pretty, but is it
                                                        Art?'

Wherefore he called to his wife, and fled to fashion his work
                                                        anew –
The first of his race who cared a fig for the first, most dread review;
And he left his lore to the use of his sons – and that was a
                                                        glorious gain
When the Devil chuckled 'Is it Art?' in the ear of the branded Cain.

They builded a tower to shiver the sky and wrench the stars apart,
Till the Devil grunted behind the bricks: 'It's striking, but is it Art?'
The stone was dropped at the quarry-side and the idle derrick
                                                        swung,

While each man talked of the aims of Art, and each in an alien
tongue.

They fought and they talked in the North and the South, they
talked and they fought in the West,
Till the waters rose on the pitiful land, and the poor Red Clay
had rest –
Had rest till that dank blank-canvas dawn when the Dove was
preened to start,
And the Devil bubbled below the keel: 'It's human, but is it Art?'

The tale is as old as the Eden Tree – and new as the new-cut tooth –
For each man knows ere his lip-thatch grows he is master of Art
and Truth;
And each man hears as the twilight nears, to the beat of his
dying heart,
The Devil drum on the darkened pane: 'You did it, but was it Art?'

We have learned to whittle the Eden Tree to the shape of a
surplice-peg,
We have learned to bottle our parents twain in the yelk of an
addled egg,
We know that the tail must wag the dog, for the horse is drawn
by the cart;
But the Devil whoops, as he whooped of old: 'It's clever, but is it
Art?'

When the flicker of London sun falls faint on the Club-room's
green and gold,
The sons of Adam sit them down and scratch with their pens in
the mould –
They scratch with their pens in the mould of their graves, and
the ink and the anguish start,
For the Devil mutters behind the leaves: 'It's pretty, but is it Art?'

Now, if we could win to the Eden Tree where the Four Great
Rivers flow,
And the Wreath of Eve is red on the turf as she left it long ago,
And if we could come when the sentry slept and softly scurry
through,
By the favour of God we might know as much – as our father
Adam knew!

# Danny Deever

'What are the bugles blowin' for?' said Files-on-Parade.
'To turn you out, to turn you out,' the Colour-Sergeant said.
'What makes you look so white, so white?' said Files-on-Parade.
'I'm dreadin' what I've got to watch,' the Colour-Sergeant said.
    For they're hangin' Danny Deever, you can hear the Dead
                                March play,
      The Regiment's in 'ollow square – they're hangin' him to-day;
      They've taken of his buttons off an' cut his stripes away,
      An' they're hangin' Danny Deever in the mornin'.

'What makes the rear-rank breathe so 'ard?' said Files-on-Parade.
'It's bitter cold, it's bitter cold,' the Colour-Sergeant said.
'What makes that front-rank man fall down?' said Files-on-Parade.
'A touch o' sun, a touch o' sun,' the Colour-Sergeant said.
    They are hangin' Danny Deever, they are marchin' of 'im
                                round,
      They 'ave 'alted Danny Deever by 'is coffin on the ground;
      An' 'e'll swing in 'arf a minute for a sneakin' shootin' hound –
      O they're hangin' Danny Deever in the mornin'!

"Is cot was right-'and cot to mine,' said Files-on-Parade.
"E's sleepin' out an' far to-night,' the Colour-Sergeant said.
'I've drunk 'is beer a score o' times,' said Files-on-Parade.
"E's drinkin' bitter beer alone,' the Colour-Sergeant said.
    They are hangin' Danny Deever, you must mark 'im to 'is
                                place,
      For 'e shot a comrade sleepin' – you must look 'im in the face;
      Nine 'undred of 'is county an' the Regiment's disgrace,
      While they're hangin' Danny Deever in the mornin'.

'What's that so black agin the sun?' said Files-on-Parade.
'It's Danny fightin' 'ard for life,' the Colour-Sergeant said.
'What's that that whimpers over'ead?' said Files-on-Parade.
'It's Danny's soul that's passin' now,' the Colour-Sergeant said.
    For they're done with Danny Deever, you can 'ear the
                                quickstep play,
      The Regiment's in column, an' they're marchin' us away;

Ho! the young recruits are shakin', an' they'll want their beer
to-day,
After hangin' Danny Deever in the mornin'.


# *Tommy*


I went into a public-'ouse to get a pint o' beer,
The publican 'e up an' sez, 'We serve no red-coats here.'
The girls be'ind the bar they laughed an' giggled fit to die,
I outs into the street again an' to myself sez I:
O it's Tommy this, an' Tommy that, an' 'Tommy, go away';
But it's 'Thank you, Mister Atkins', when the band begins
to play,
The band begins to play, my boys, the band begins to play,
O it's 'Thank you, Mister Atkins', when the band begins to
play.

I went into a theatre as sober as could be,
They gave a drunk civilian room, but 'adn't none for me;
They sent me to the gallery or round the music-'alls,
But when it comes to fightin', Lord! they'll shove me in the stalls!
For it's Tommy this, an' Tommy that, an' 'Tommy, wait
outside';
But it's 'Special train for Atkins' when the trooper's on the
tide –
The troopship's on the tide, my boys, the troopship's on
the tide,
O it's 'Special train for Atkins' when the trooper's on the
tide.

Yes, makin' mock o' uniforms that guard you while you sleep
Is cheaper than them uniforms, an' they're starvation cheap;
An' hustlin' drunken soldiers when they're goin' large a bit
Is five times better business than paradin' in full kit.
  Then it's Tommy this, an' Tommy that, an' 'Tommy, 'ow's
                yer soul?'
  But it's 'Thin red line of 'eroes' when the drums begin to
                roll,
  The drums begin to roll, my boys, the drums begin to roll,
  O it's 'Thin red line of 'eroes' when the drums begin to roll.

We aren't no thin red 'eroes, nor we aren't no blackguards too,
But single men in barricks, most remarkable like you;
An' if sometimes our conduck isn't all your fancy paints,
Why, single men in barricks don't grow into plaster saints;
  While it's Tommy this, an' Tommy that, an' 'Tommy,
                fall be'ind',
  But it's 'Please to walk in front, sir', when there's trouble
                in the wind,
  There's trouble in the wind, my boys, there's trouble in
                the wind,
  O it's 'Please to walk in front, sir', when there's trouble in
                the wind.

You talk o' better food for us, an' schools, an' fires, an' all:
We'll wait for extry rations if you treat us rational.
Don't mess about the cook-room slops, but prove it to our face
The Widow's Uniform is not the soldier-man's disgrace.
  For it's Tommy this, an' Tommy that, an' 'Chuck him
              out, the brute!'
  But it's 'Saviour of 'is country' when the guns begin to
                shoot;
  An' it's Tommy this, an' Tommy that, an' anything you
                please;
  An' Tommy ain't a bloomin' fool – you bet that Tommy
                sees!

# The Widow at Windsor

'Ave you 'eard o' the Widow at Windsor
    With a hairy gold crown on 'er 'ead?
She 'as ships on the foam – she 'as millions at 'ome,
    An' she pays us poor beggars in red.
        (Ow, poor beggars in red!)
There's 'er nick on the cavalry 'orses,
    There's 'er mark on the medical stores –
An' 'er troopers you'll find with a fair wind be'ind
    That takes us to various wars.
        (Poor beggars! – barbarious wars!)
        Then 'ere's to the Widow at Windsor,
            An' 'ere's to the stores an' the guns,
        The men an' the 'orses what makes up the forces
            O' Missis Victorier's sons.
        (Poor beggars! Victorier's sons!)

Walk wide o' the Widow at Windsor,
    For 'alf o' Creation she owns:
We 'ave bought 'er the same with the sword an' the flame,
    An' we've salted it down with our bones.
        (Poor beggars! – it's blue with our bones!)
Hands off o' the sons o' the Widow,
    Hands off o' the goods in 'er shop,
For the Kings must come down an' the Emperors frown
    When the Widow at Windsor says 'Stop'!
        (Poor beggars! – we're sent to say 'Stop'!)
        Then 'ere's to the Lodge o' the Widow,
            From the Pole to the Tropics it runs –
        To the Lodge that we tile with the rank an' the file,
            An' open in form with the guns.
        (Poor beggars! – it's always they guns!)

We 'ave 'eard o' the Widow at Windsor,
    It's safest to let 'er alone:
For 'er sentries we stand by the sea an' the land
    Wherever the bugles are blown.
        (Poor beggars! – an' don't we get blown!)
Take 'old o' the Wings o' the Mornin',
    An' flop round the earth till you're dead;
But you won't get away from the tune that they play
    To the bloomin' old rag over'ead.
        (Poor beggars! – it's 'ot over'ead!)
            Then 'ere's to the sons o' the Widow,
                Wherever, 'owever they roam.
            'Ere's all they desire, an' if they require
                A speedy return to their 'ome.
            (Poor beggars! – they'll never see 'ome!)


## Gunga Din


You may talk o' gin and beer
When you're quartered safe out 'ere,
An' you're sent to penny-fights an' Aldershot it;
But when it comes to slaughter
You will do your work on water,
An' you'll lick the bloomin' boots of 'im that's got it.
Now in Injia's sunny clime,
Where I used to spend my time
A-servin' of 'Er Majesty the Queen,
Of all them blackfaced crew
The finest man I knew
Was our regimental bhisti, Gunga Din.
            He was 'Din! Din! Din!
        You limpin' lump o' brick-dust, Gunga Din!
            Hi! Slippy *hitherao*!
            Water, get it! *Panee lao*!
        You squidgy-nosed old idol, Gunga Din.'

The uniform 'e wore
Was nothin' much before,
An' rather less than 'arf o' that be'ind,
For a piece o' twisty rag
An' a goatskin water-bag
Was all the field-equipment 'e could find.
When the sweatin' troop-train lay
In a sidin' through the day,
Where the 'eat would make your bloomin' eyebrows crawl,
We shouted 'Harry By!'
Till our throats were bricky-dry,
Then we wopped 'im 'cause 'e couldn't serve us all.
      It was 'Din! Din! Din!
  You 'eathen, where the mischief 'ave you been?
     You put some *juldee* in it
     Or I'll *marrow* you this minute
  If you don't fill up my helmet, Gunga Din!'

'E would dot an' carry one
Till the longest day was done;
An' 'e didn't seem to know the use o' fear.
If we charged or broke or cut,
You could bet your bloomin' nut,
'E'd be waitin' fifty paces right flank rear.
With 'is *mussick* on 'is back,
'E would skip with our attack,
An' watch us till the bugles made 'Retire',
An' for all 'is dirty 'ide
'E was white, clear white, inside
When 'e went to tend the wounded under fire!
      It was 'Din! Din! Din!'
  With the bullets kickin' dust-spots on the green.
     When the cartridges ran out,
     You could hear the front-ranks shout,
  'Hi! ammunition-mules an' Gunga Din!'

I shan't forgit the night
When I dropped be'ind the fight
With a bullet where my belt-plate should 'a' been.
I was chokin' mad with thirst,
An' the man that spied me first
Was our good old grinnin', gruntin' Gunga Din.
'E lifted up my 'ead,
An' he plugged me where I bled,
An' 'e guv me 'arf-a-pint o' water-green:
It was crawlin' and it stunk,
But of all the drinks I've drunk,
I'm gratefullest to one from Gunga Din.
        It was 'Din! Din! Din!
   'Ere's a beggar with a bullet through 'is spleen;
      'E's chawin' up the ground,
      An' 'e's kickin' all around:
   For Gawd's sake git the water, Gunga Din!'

'E carried me away
To where a dooli lay,
An' a bullet come an' drilled the beggar clean.
'E put me safe inside,
An' just before 'e died,
'I 'ope you liked your drink,' sez Gunga Din.
So I'll meet 'im later on
At the place where 'e is gone –
Where it's always double drill and no canteen.
'E'll be squattin' on the coals
Givin' drink to poor damned souls,
An' I'll get a swig in hell from Gunga Din!
        Yes, Din! Din! Din!
   You Lazarushian-leather Gunga Din!
      Though I've belted you and flayed you,
      By the livin' Gawd that made you,
  You're a better man than I am, Gunga Din!

# Mandalay

By the old Moulmein Pagoda, lookin' eastward to the sea,
There's a Burma girl a-settin', and I know she thinks o' me;
For the wind is in the palm-trees, and the temple-bells they say:
'Come you back, you British soldier; come you back to Mandalay!'
    Come you back to Mandalay,
    Where the old Flotilla lay:
    Can't you 'ear their paddles chunkin' from Rangoon to
                Mandalay?
    On the road to Mandalay,
    Where the flyin'-fishes play,
    An' the dawn comes up like thunder outer China 'crost
                the Bay!

'Er petticoat was yaller an' 'er little cap was green,
An' 'er name was Supi-yaw-lat – jes' the same as Theebaw's Queen,
An' I seed her first a-smokin' of a whackin' white cheroot,
An' a-wastin' Christian kisses on an 'eathen idol's foot:
    Bloomin' idol made o' mud –
    Wot they called the Great Gawd Budd –
    Plucky lot she cared for idols when I kissed 'er where she
                stud!
    On the road to Mandalay ...

When the mist was on the rice-fields an' the sun was droppin' slow,
She'd git 'er little banjo an' she'd sing 'Kulla-lo-lo!'
With 'er arm upon my shoulder an' 'er cheek agin' my cheek
We useter watch the steamers an' the *hathis* pilin' teak.
    Elephints a-pilin' teak
    In the sludgy, squdgy creek,
    Where the silence 'ung that 'eavy you was 'arf afraid to
                speak!
    On the road to Mandalay ...

But that's all shove be'ind me – long ago an' fur away,
An' there ain't no 'buses runnin' from the Bank to Mandalay;
An' I'm learnin' 'ere in London what the ten-year soldier tells:
'If you've 'eard the East a-callin', you won't never 'eed naught
else.'

    No! you won't 'eed nothin' else
    But them spicy garlic smells,
    An' the sunshine an' the palm-trees an' the tinkly
temple-bells;
    On the road to Mandalay …

I am sick o' wastin' leather on these gritty pavin'-stones,
An' the blasted Henglish drizzle wakes the fever in my bones;
Tho' I walks with fifty 'ousemaids outer Chelsea to the Strand,
An' they talks a lot o' lovin', but wot do they understand?
    Beefy face an' grubby 'and –
    Law! wot do they understand?
    I've a neater, sweeter maiden in a cleaner, greener land!
    On the road to Mandalay …

Ship me somewheres east of Suez, where the best is like the worst,
Where there aren't no Ten Commandments an' a man can raise a
thirst;
For the temple-bells are callin', an' it's there that I would be –
By the old Moulmein Pagoda, looking lazy at the sea;
    On the road to Mandalay,
    Where the old Flotilla lay,
    With our sick beneath the awnings when we went to
Mandalay!
    On the road to Mandalay,
    Where the flyin'-fishes play,
    An' the dawn comes up like thunder outer China 'crost
the Bay!

# The Young British Soldier

When the 'arf-made recruity goes out to the East
'E acts like a babe an' 'e drinks like a beast,
An' 'e wonders because 'e is frequent deceased
    Ere 'e's fit for to serve as a soldier.
      Serve, serve, serve as a soldier,
      Serve, serve, serve as a soldier,
      Serve, serve, serve as a soldier,
        So-oldier *of* the Queen!

Now all you recruities what's drafted to-day,
You shut up your rag-box an' 'ark to my lay,
An' I'll sing you a soldier as far as I may:
    A soldier what's fit for a soldier.
      Fit, fit, fit for a soldier …

First mind you steer clear o' the grog-sellers' huts,
For they sell you Fixed Bay'nets that rots out your guts –
Ay, drink that 'ud eat the live steel from your butts –
    An' it's bad for the young British soldier.
      Bad, bad, bad for the soldier …

When the cholera comes – as it will past a doubt –
Keep out of the wet and don't go on the shout,
For the sickness gets in as the liquor dies out,
    An' it crumples the young British soldier.
      Crum-, crum-, crumples the soldier …

But the worst o' your foes is the sun over'ead:
You *must* wear your 'elmet for all that is said:
If 'e finds you uncovered 'e'll knock you down dead,
    An' you'll die like a fool of a soldier.
      Fool, fool, fool of a soldier …

If you're cast for fatigue by a sergeant unkind,
Don't grouse like a woman nor crack on nor blind;
Be handy and civil, and then you will find
    That it's beer for the young British soldier.
      Beer, beer, beer for the soldier …

Now, if you must marry, take care she is old –
A troop-sergeant's widow's the nicest I'm told,
For beauty won't help if your rations is cold,
    Nor love ain't enough for a soldier.
      'Nough, 'nough, 'nough for a soldier ...

If the wife should go wrong with a comrade, be loth
To shoot when you catch 'em – you'll swing, on my oath! –
Make 'im take 'er and keep 'er: that's Hell for them both,
    An' you're shut o' the curse of a soldier.
      Curse, curse, curse of a soldier ...

When first under fire an' you're wishful to duck,
Don't look nor take 'eed at the man that is struck,
Be thankful you're livin', and trust to your luck
    And march to your front like a soldier.
      Front, front, front like a soldier ...

When 'arf of your bullets fly wide in the ditch,
Don't call your Martini a cross-eyed old bitch;
She's human as you are – you treat her as sich,
    An' she'll fight for the young British soldier.
      Fight, fight, fight for the soldier ...

When shakin' their bustles like ladies so fine,
The guns o' the enemy wheel into line,
Shoot low at the limbers an' don't mind the shine,
    For noise never startles the soldier.
      Start-, start-, startles the soldier ...

If your officer's dead and the sergeants look white,
Remember it's ruin to run from a fight:
So take open order, lie down, and sit tight,
    And wait for supports like a soldier.
      Wait, wait, wait like a soldier ...

When you're wounded and left on Afghanistan's plains,
And the women come out to cut up what remains,
Jest roll to your rifle and blow out your brains
    An' go to your Gawd like a soldier.
      Go, go, go like a soldier,
      Go, go, go like a soldier,
      Go, go, go like a soldier,
        So-oldier *of* the Queen!

## The Last of the Light Brigade
### 1891

There were thirty million English who talked of England's might,
There were twenty broken troopers who lacked a bed for the night.
They had neither food nor money, they had neither service nor
                              trade;
They were only shiftless soldiers, the last of the Light Brigade.

They felt that life was fleeting; they knew not that art was long,
That though they were dying of famine, they lived in deathless
                              song.
They asked for a little money to keep the wolf from the door;
And the thirty million English sent twenty pounds and four!

They laid their heads together that were scarred and lined and
                              grey;
Keen were the Russian sabres, but want was keener than they;
And an old Troop-Sergeant muttered, 'Let us go to the man who
                              writes
The things on Balaclava the kiddies at school recites.'

They went without bands or colours, a regiment ten-file strong,
To look for the Master-singer who had crowned them all in his
                              song;
And, waiting his servant's order, by the garden gate they stayed,
A desolate little cluster, the last of the Light Brigade.

They strove to stand to attention, to straighten the toil-bowed back;
They drilled on an empty stomach, the loose-knit files fell slack;
With stooping of weary shoulders, in garments tattered and
                                                                                                frayed,
They shambled into his presence, the last of the Light Brigade.

The old Troop-Sergeant was spokesman, and 'Beggin' your
                                                                                        pardon,' he said,
'You wrote o' the Light Brigade, sir. Here's all that isn't dead.
An' it's all come true what you wrote, sir, regardin' the mouth of
                                                                                                        hell;
For we're all of us nigh to the workhouse, an' we thought we'd
                                                                                        call an' tell.

'No, thank you, we don't want food, sir; but couldn't you take
                                                                                        an' write
A sort of "to be continued" and "see next page" o' the fight?
We think that someone has blundered, an' couldn't you tell 'em
                                                                                        how?
You wrote we were heroes once, sir. Please, write we are
                                                                                        starving now.'

The poor little army departed, limping and lean and forlorn.
And the heart of the Master-singer grew hot with 'the scorn of
                                                                                        scorn'.
And he wrote for them wonderful verses that swept the land
                                                                                        like flame,
Till the fatted souls of the English were scourged with the thing
                                                                                        called Shame.


O thirty million English that babble of England's might,
Behold there are twenty heroes who lack their food to-night;
Our children's children are lisping to 'honour the charge they
                                                                                        made' –
And we leave to the streets and the workhouse the charge of the
                                                                                        Light Brigade!

# Tomlinson

## 1891

Now Tomlinson gave up the ghost in his house in Berkeley Square,
And a Spirit came to his bedside and gripped him by the hair –
A Spirit gripped him by the hair and carried him far away,
Till he heard as the roar of a rain-fed ford the roar of the Milky
                                                                    Way:
Till he heard the roar of the Milky Way die down and drone and
                                                                    cease,
And they came to the Gate within the Wall where Peter holds
                                                                    the keys.
'Stand up, stand up now, Tomlinson, and answer loud and high
The good that ye did for the sake of men or ever ye came to die –
The good that ye did for the sake of men on little Earth so lone!'
And the naked soul of Tomlinson grew white as a rain-washed
                                                                    bone.

'O I have a friend on Earth,' he said, 'that was my priest and
                                                                    guide,
And well would he answer all for me if he were by my side.'
– 'For that ye strove in neighbour-love it shall be written fair,
But now ye wait at Heaven's Gate and not in Berkeley Square:
Though we called your friend from his bed this night, he could
                                                                    not speak for you,
For the race is run by one and one and never by two and two.'
Then Tomlinson looked up and down, and little gain was there,
For the naked stars grinned overhead, and he saw that his soul
                                                                    was bare.
The Wind that blows between the worlds, it cut him like a knife,
And Tomlinson took up his tale and spoke of his good in life.
'O this I have read in a book,' he said, 'and that was told to me,
And this I have thought that another man thought of a Prince in
                                                                    Muscovy.'
The good souls flocked like homing doves and bade him clear
                                                                    the path,
And Peter twirled the jangling keys in weariness and wrath.
'Ye have read, ye have heard, ye have thought,' he said, 'and the
                                                                    tale is yet to run:

By the worth of the body that once ye had, give answer – what
ha' ye done?'
Then Tomlinson looked back and forth, and little good it bore,
For the Darkness stayed at his shoulder-blade and Heaven's
Gate before: –
'O this I have felt, and this I have guessed, and this I have heard
men say,
And this they wrote that another man wrote of a carl in Norroway.'
– 'Ye have read, ye have felt, ye have guessed, good lack! Ye
have hampered Heaven's Gate;
There's little room between the stars in idleness to prate!
O none may reach by hired speech of neighbour, priest, and kin
Through borrowed deed to God's good meed that lies so fair
within;
Get hence, get hence to the Lord of Wrong, for doom has yet to
run,
And ... the faith that ye share with Berkeley Square uphold you,
Tomlinson!'

*

The Spirit gripped him by the hair, and sun by sun they fell
Till they came to the belt of Naughty Stars that rim the mouth of
Hell:
The first are red with pride and wrath, the next are white with pain,
But the third are black with clinkered sin that cannot burn again:
They may hold their path, they may leave their path, with never
a soul to mark:
They may burn or freeze, but they must not cease in the Scorn of
the Outer Dark.
The Wind that blows between the worlds, it nipped him to the
bone,
And he yearned to the flare of Hell-Gate there as the light of his
own hearth-stone.
The Devil he sat behind the bars, where the desperate legions
drew,
But he caught the hasting Tomlinson and would not let him
through.
'Wot ye the price of good pit-coal that I must pay?' said he,
'That ye rank yoursel' so fit for Hell and ask no leave of me?
I am all o'er-sib to Adam's breed that ye should give me scorn,

For I strove with God for your First Father the day that he was
born.

Sit down, sit down upon the slag, and answer loud and high
The harm that ye did to the Sons of Men or ever you came to die.'
And Tomlinson looked up and up, and saw against the night
The belly of a tortured star blood-red in Hell-Mouth light;
And Tomlinson looked down and down, and saw beneath his feet
The frontlet of a tortured star milk-white in Hell-Mouth heat.
'O I had a love on earth,' said he, 'that kissed me to my fall,
And if ye would call my love to me I know she would answer all.'
– 'All that ye did in love forbid it shall be written fair,
But now ye wait at Hell-Mouth Gate and not in Berkeley Square:
Though we whistled your love from her bed to-night, I trow she
would not run,

For the sin ye do by two and two ye must pay for one by one!'
The Wind that blows between the worlds, it cut him like a knife,
And Tomlinson took up the tale and spoke of his sins in life: –
'Once I ha' laughed at the power of Love and twice at the grip of
the Grave,

And thrice I ha' patted my God on the head that men might call
me brave.'

The Devil he blew on a brandered soul and set it aside to cool: –
'Do ye think I would waste my good pit-coal on the hide of a
brain-sick fool?

I see no worth in the hobnailed mirth or the jolthead jest ye did
That I should waken my gentlemen that are sleeping three on a
grid.'

Then Tomlinson looked back and forth, and there was little grace,
For Hell-Gate filled the houseless Soul with the Fear of Naked
Space.

'Nay, this I ha' heard,' quo' Tomlinson, 'and this was noised
abroad,

And this I ha' got from a Belgian book on the word of a dead
French lord.'

– 'Ye ha' heard, ye ha' read, ye ha' got, good lack! and the tale
begins afresh –

Have ye sinned one sin for the pride o' the eye or the sinful lust
of the flesh?'

Then Tomlinson he gripped the bars and yammered, 'Let me in –
For I mind that I borrowed my neighbour's wife to sin the
deadly sin.'

The Devil he grinned behind the bars, and banked the fires high:
'Did ye read of that sin in a book?' said he; and Tomlinson said,
                                                            'Ay!'
The Devil he blew upon his nails, and the little devils ran,
And he said: 'Go husk this whimpering thief that comes in the
                                        guise of a man:
Winnow him out 'twixt star and star, and sieve his proper worth:
There's sore decline in Adam's line if this be spawn of earth.'
Empusa's crew, so naked-new they may not face the fire,
But weep that they bin too small to sin to the height of their desire,
Over the coal they chased the Soul, and racked it all abroad,
As children rifle a caddis-case or the raven's foolish hoard.
And back they came with the tattered Thing, as children after play,
And they said: 'The soul that he got from God he has bartered
                                        clean away.
We have threshed a stook of print and book, and winnowed a
                                        chattering wind
And many a soul wherefrom he stole, but his we cannot find.
We have handled him, we have dandled him, we have seared
                                        him to the bone,
And sure if tooth and nail show truth he has no soul of his own.'
The Devil he bowed his head on his breast and rumbled deep
                                        and low: –
'I'm all o'er-sib to Adam's breed that I should bid him go.
Yet close we lie, and deep we lie, and if I gave him place,
My gentlemen that are so proud would flout me to my face;
They'd call my house a common stews and me a careless host,
And – I would not anger my gentlemen for the sake of a shiftless
                                        ghost.'
The Devil he looked at the mangled Soul that prayed to feel the
                                        flame,
And he thought of Holy Charity, but he thought of his own
                                        good name: –
'Now ye could haste my coal to waste, and sit ye down to fry:
Did ye think of that theft for yourself?' said he; and Tomlinson
                                        said, 'Ay!'
The Devil he blew an outward breath, for his heart was free
                                        from care: –
'Ye have scarce the soul of a louse,' he said, 'but the roots of sin
                                        are there,
And for that sin should ye come in were I the lord alone,

But sinful pride has rule inside – and mightier than my own.
Honour and Wit, fore-damned they sit, to each his priest and
                                                          whore;
Nay, scarce I dare myself go there, and you they'd torture sore.
Ye are neither spirit nor spirk,' he said; 'ye are neither book nor
                                                          brute –
Go, get ye back to the flesh again for the sake of Man's repute.
I'm all o'er-sib to Adam's breed that I should mock your pain,
But look that ye win to worthier sin ere ye come back again.
Get hence, the hearse is at your door – the grim black stallions
                                                          wait –
They bear your clay to place to-day. Speed, lest ye come too
                                                          late!
Go back to Earth with a lip unsealed – go back with an open eye,
And carry my word to the Sons of Men or ever ye come to die:
That the sin they do by two and two they must pay for one by
                                                          one –
And ... the God that you took from a printed book be with you,
                                                          Tomlinson!'


## The Long Trail


There's a whisper down the field where the year has shot her yield,
    And the ricks stand grey to the sun,
Singing: 'Over then, come over, for the bee has quit the clover,
    And your English summer's done.'
        You have heard the beat of the off-shore wind,
        And the thresh of the deep-sea rain;
        You have heard the song – how long? how long?
        Pull out on the trail again!

            Ha' done with the Tents of Shem, dear lass,
            We've seen the seasons through,
            And it's time to turn on the old trail, our own trail, the
                                                          out trail,
            Pull out, pull out, on the Long Trail – the trail that is
                                                          always new!

It's North you may run to the rime-ringed sun
  Or South to the blind Horn's hate;
Or East all the way into Mississippi Bay,
  Or West to the Golden Gate –
    Where the blindest bluffs hold good, dear lass,
    And the wildest tales are true,
    And the men bulk big on the old trail, our own trail, the out
                                                          trail,
    And life runs large on the Long Trail – the trail that is
                                              always new.

The days are sick and cold, and the skies are grey and old,
  And the twice-breathed airs blow damp;
And I'd sell my tired soul for the bucking beam-sea roll
  Of a black Bilbao tramp,
    With her load-line over her hatch, dear lass,
    And a drunken Dago crew,
    And her nose held down on the old trail, our own trail, the
                                                      out trail
    From Cadiz south on the Long Trail – the trail that is
                                              always new.

There be triple ways to take, of the eagle or the snake,
  Or the way of a man with a maid;
But the sweetest way to me is a ship's upon the sea
  In the heel of the North-East Trade.
    Can you hear the crash on her brows, dear lass.
    And the drum of the racing screw,
    As she ships it green on the old trail, our own trail, the out
                                                          trail,
    As she lifts and 'scends on the Long Trail – the trail that is
                                              always new?

See the shaking funnels roar, with the Peter at the fore,
  And the fenders grind and heave,
And the derricks clack and grate, as the tackle hooks the crate,
  And the fall-rope whines through the sheave;
    It's 'Gang-plank up and in', dear lass,
    It's 'Hawsers warp her through!'
    And it's 'All clear aft' on the old trail, our own trail, the out
                                                          trail,
    We're backing down on the Long Trail – the trail that is
                                              always new.

O the mutter overside, when the port-fog holds us tied,
   And the sirens hoot their dread,
When foot by foot we creep o'er the hueless, viewless deep
    To the sob of the questing lead!
      It's down by the Lower Hope, dear lass,
      With the Gunfleet Sands in view,
      Till the Mouse swings green on the old trail, our own trail,
               the out trail,
      And the Gull Light lifts on the Long Trail – the trail that is
               always new.


O the blazing tropic night, when the wake's a welt of light
   That holds the hot sky tame,
And the steady fore-foot snores through the planet-powdered
                       floors
   Where the scared whale flukes in flame!
      Her plates are flaked by the sun, dear lass
      And her ropes are taut with the dew,
      For we're booming down on the old trail, our own trail, the
               out trail,
      We're sagging south on the Long Trail – the trail that is
               always new.


Then home, get her home, where the drunken rollers comb,
   And the shouting seas drive by,
And the engines stamp and ring, and the wet bows reel and swing,
   And the Southern Cross rides high!
      Yes, the old lost stars wheel back, dear lass,
      That blaze in the velvet blue.
      They're all old friends on the old trail, our own trail, the out
               trail,
      They're God's own guides on the Long Trail – the trail that
               is always new.


Fly forward, O my heart, from the Foreland to the Start –
   We're steaming all too slow,
And it's twenty thousand mile to our little lazy isle
   Where the trumpet-orchids blow!
      You have heard the call of the off-shore wind
      And the voice of the deep-sea rain;
      You have heard the song – how long? – how long?
      Pull out on the trail again!

The Lord knows what we may find, dear lass,
And The Deuce knows what we may do –
But we're back once more on the old trail, our own trail, the out
trail,
We're down, hull-down, on the Long Trail – the trail that is
always new!


## The Song of the Galley-Slaves

*('The Finest Story in the World'* – Many Inventions)


We pulled for you when the wind was against us and the sails
were low.
*Will you never let us go?*
We ate bread and onions when you took towns, or ran aboard
quickly when you were beaten back by the foe.
The Captains walked up and down the deck in fair weather
singing songs, but we were below.
We fainted with our chins on the oars and you did not see that we
were idle, for we still swung to and fro.
*Will you never let us go?*
The salt made the oar-handles like shark-skin; our knees were
cut to the bone with salt-cracks; our hair was stuck to our
foreheads; and our lips were cut to the gums, and you
whipped us because we could not row.
*Will you never let us go?*
But, in a little time, we shall run out of the port-holes as the water
runs along the oar-blade, and though you tell the others
to row after us you will never catch us till you catch the
oar-thresh and tie up the winds in the belly of the sail. Aho!
*Will you never let us go?*

# McAndrew's Hymn
## 1893

Lord, Thou hast made this world below the shadow of a dream,
An', taught by time, I tak' it so – exceptin' always Steam.
From coupler-flange to spindle-guide I see Thy Hand, O God –
Predestination in the stride o' yon connectin'-rod.
John Calvin might ha' forged the same – enorrmous, certain, slow –
Ay, wrought it in the furnace-flame – *my* 'Institutio'.
I cannot get my sleep to-night; old bones are hard to please;
I'll stand the middle watch up here – alone wi' God an' these
My engines, after ninety days o' race an' rack an' strain
Through all the seas of all Thy world, slam-bangin' home again.
Slam-bang too much – they knock a wee – the crosshead-gibs are
loose,
But thirty thousand mile o' sea has gied them fair excuse …
Fine, clear an' dark – a full-draught breeze, wi' Ushant out o' sight,
An' Ferguson relievin' Hay. Old girl, ye'll walk to-night!
His wife's at Plymouth … Seventy – One – Two – Three since he
began –
Three turns for Mistress Ferguson … and who's to blame the man?
There's none at any port for me, by drivin' fast or slow,
Since Elsie Campbell went to Thee, Lord, thirty years ago.
(The year the *Sarah Sands* was burned. Oh, roads we used to tread,
Fra' Maryhill to Pollokshaws – fra' Govan to Parkhead!)
Not but they're ceevil on the Board. Ye'll hear Sir Kenneth say:
'Good morrn, McAndrew! Back again? An' how's your bilge
to-day?'
Miscallin' technicalities but handin' me my chair
To drink Madeira wi' three Earls – the auld Fleet Engineer
That started as a boiler-whelp – when steam and he were low.
*I* mind the time we used to serve a broken pipe wi' tow!
Ten pound was all the pressure then – Eh! Eh! – a man wad drive;
An' here, our workin' gauges give one hunder sixty-five!
We're creepin' on wi' each new rig – less weight an' larger power;
There'll be the loco-boiler next an' thirty mile an hour!
Thirty an' more. What I ha' seen since ocean-steam began
Leaves me na doot for the machine: but what about the man?

The man that counts, wi' all his runs, one million mile o' sea:
Four time the span from earth to moon ... How far, O Lord,
                                                    from Thee
That wast beside him night an' day? Ye mind my first typhoon?
It scoughed the skipper on his way to jock wi' the saloon.
Three feet were on the stokehold-floor – just slappin' to an' fro –
An' cast me on a furnace-door. I have the marks to show.
Marks! I ha' marks o' more than burns – deep in my soul an' black,
An' times like this, when things go smooth, my wickudness
                                                    comes back.
The sins o' four an' forty years, all up an' down the seas,
Clack an' repeat like valves half-fed ... Forgie's our trespasses!
Nights when I'd come on deck to mark, wi' envy in my gaze,
The couples kittlin' in the dark between the funnel-stays;
Years when I raked the Ports wi' pride to fill my cup o' wrong –
Judge not, O Lord, my steps aside at Gay Street in Hong-Kong!
Blot out the wastrel hours of mine in sin when I abode –
Jane Harrigan's an' Number Nine, The Reddick an' Grant Road!
An' waur than all – my crownin' sin – rank blasphemy an' wild.
I was not four and twenty then – Ye wadna judge a child?
I'd seen the tropics first that run – new fruit, new smells, new air –
How could I tell – blind-fou wi' sun – the Deil was lurkin' there?
By day like playhouse-scenes the shore slid past our sleepy eyes;
By night those soft, lasceevious stars leered from those velvet
                                                    skies,
In port (we used no cargo-steam) I'd daunder down the streets –
An ijjit grinnin' in a dream – for shells an' parrakeets,
An' walkin'-sticks o' carved bamboo an' blowfish stuffed an'
                                                    dried –
Fillin' my bunk wi' rubbishry the Chief put overside.
Till, off Sambawa Head, Ye mind, I heard a land-breeze ca',
Milk-warm wi' breath o' spice an' bloom: 'McAndrew, come
                                                    awa'!'
Firm, clear an' low – no haste, no hate – the ghostly whisper
                                                    went,
Just statin' eevidential facts beyon' all argument:
'Your mither's God's a graspin' deil, the shadow o' yoursel';
Got out o' books by meenisters clean daft on Heaven an' Hell.
They mak' him in the Broomielaw, o' Glasgie cold an' dirt,
A jealous, pridefu' fetich, lad, that's only strong to hurt.
Ye'll not go back to Him again an' kiss His red-hot rod,

But come wi' Us' (Now, who were *They*?) 'an' know the Leevin'
                                                                God,
That does not kipper souls for sport or break a life in jest,
But swells the ripenin' cocoanuts an' ripes the woman's breast.'
An' there it stopped – cut off – no more – that quiet, certain
                                                                voice –
For me, six months o' twenty-four, to leave or take at choice.
'Twas on me like a thunderclap – it racked me through an'
                                                                through –
Temptation past the show o' speech, unnameable an' new –
The Sin against the Holy Ghost? … An' under all, our screw.

                                *

That storm blew by but left behind her anchor-shiftin' swell.
Thou knowest all my heart an' mind, Thou knowest, Lord, I fell –
Third on the *Mary Gloster* then, and first that night in Hell!
Yet was Thy Hand beneath my head, about my feet Thy Care –
Fra' Deli clear to Torres Strait, the trial o' despair,
But when we touched the Barrier Reef Thy answer to my prayer! …
We dared na run that sea by night but lay an' held our fire,
An' I was drowsin' on the hatch – sick – sick – wi' doubt an' tire:
*'Better the sight of eyes that see than wanderin' o' desire!'*
Ye mind that word? Clear as our gongs – again, an' once again,
When rippin' down through coral-trash ran out our moorin'-
                                                                chain:
An', by Thy Grace, I had the Light to see my duty plain.
Light on the engine-room – no more – bright as our carbons burn.
I've lost it since a thousand times, but never past return!

                                *

Obsairve! Per annum we'll have here two thousand souls aboard –
Think not I dare to justify myself before the Lord,
But – average fifteen hunder souls safe-borne fra' port to port –
I *am* o' service to my kind. Ye wadna blame the thought?
Maybe they steam from Grace to Wrath – to sin by folly led –
It isna mine to judge their path – their lives are on my head.
Mine at the last – when all is done it all comes back to me,
The fault that leaves six thousand ton a log upon the sea.
We'll tak' one stretch – three weeks an' odd by ony road ye steer –

                                63

Fra' Cape Town east to Wellington – ye need an engineer.
Fail there – ye've time to weld your shaft – ay, eat it, ere ye're
spoke;
Or make Kerguelen under sail – three jiggers burned wi' smoke!
An' home again – the Rio run: it's no child's play to go
Steamin' to bell for fourteen days o' snow an' floe an' blow.
The bergs like kelpies overside that girn an' turn an' shift
Whaur, grindin' like the Mills o' God, goes by the big South drift.
(Hail, Snow and Ice that praise the Lord. I've met them at their
work,
An' wished we had anither route or they anither kirk.)
Yon's strain, hard strain, o' head an' hand, for though Thy
Power brings
All skill to naught, Ye'll understand a man must think o' things.
Then, at the last, we'll get to port an' hoist their baggage clear –
The passengers, wi' gloves an' canes – an' this is what I'll hear:
'Well, thank ye for a pleasant voyage. The tender's comin' now.'
While I go testin' follower-bolts an' watch the skipper bow.
They've words for every one but me – shake hands wi' half the
crew,
Except the dour Scots engineer, the man they never knew.
An' yet I like the wark for all we've dam'-few pickin's here –
No pension, an' the most we'll earn's four hunder pound a year.
Better myself abroad? Maybe. *I'd* sooner starve than sail
Wi' such as call a snifter-rod *ross* ... French for nightingale.
Commeesion on my stores? Some do; but I cannot afford
To lie like stewards wi' patty-pans. I'm older than the Board.
A bonus on the coal I save? Ou ay, the Scots are close,
But when I grudge the strength Ye gave I'll grudge their food to
*those*.
(There's bricks that I might recommend – an' clink the fire-bars
cruel.
No! Welsh – Wangarti at the worst – an' damn all patent fuel!)
Inventions? Ye must stay in port to mak' a patent pay.
My Deeferential Valve-Gear taught me how that business lay.
I blame no chaps wi' clearer heads for aught they make or sell.
*I* found that I could not invent an' look to these as well.
So, wrestled wi' Apollyon – Nah! – fretted like a bairn –
But burned the workin'-plans last run, wi' all I hoped to earn.
Ye know how hard an Idol dies, an' what that meant to me –
E'en tak' it for a sacrifice acceptable to Thee ...

*Below there! Oiler! What's your wark? Ye find it runnin' hard?*
*Ye needn't swill the cup wi' oil – this isn't the Cunard!*
*Ye thought? Ye are not paid to think. Go, sweat that off again!*
Tck! Tck! It's deeficult to sweer nor tak' The Name in vain!
Men, ay, an' women, call me stern. Wi' these to oversee,
Ye'll note I've little time to burn on social repartee.
The bairns see what their elders miss; they'll hunt me to an' fro,
Till for the sake of – well, a kiss – I tak' 'em down below.
That minds me of our Viscount loon – Sir Kenneth's kin – the chap
Wi' Russia-leather tennis-shoon an' spar-decked yachtin'-cap.
I showed him round last week, o'er all – an' at the last says he:
'Mister McAndrew, don't you think steam spoils romance at sea?'
Damned ijjit! I'd been doon that morn to see what ailed the throws,
Manholin', on my back – the cranks three inches off my nose.
Romance! Those first-class passengers they like it very well,
Printed an' bound in little books; but why don't poets tell?
I'm sick of all their quirks an' turns – the loves an' doves they
                                                    dream –
Lord, send a man like Robbie Burns to sing the Song o' Steam!
To match wi' Scotia's noblest speech yon orchestra sublime
Whaurto – uplifted like the Just – the tail-rods mark the time.
The crank-throws give the double-bass, the feed-pump sobs an'
                                                    heaves,
An' now the main eccentrics start their quarrel on the sheaves:
Her time, her own appointed time, the rocking link-head bides,
Till – hear that note? – the rod's return whings glimmerin'
                                                    through the guides.
They're all awa'! True beat, full power, the clangin' chorus goes
Clear to the tunnel where they sit, my purrin' dynamoes.
Interdependence absolute, foreseen, ordained, decreed,
To work, Ye'll note, at ony tilt an' every rate o' speed.
Fra' skylight-lift to furnace-bars, backed, bolted, braced an' stayed,
An' singin' like the Mornin' Stars for joy that they are made;
While, out o' touch o' vanity, the sweatin' thrust-block says:
'Not unto us the praise, or man – not unto us the praise!'
Now, a' together, hear them lift their lesson – theirs an' mine:
'Law, Orrder, Duty an' Restraint, Obedience, Discipline!'
Mill, forge an' try-pit taught them that when roarin' they arose,
An' whiles I wonder if a soul was gied them wi' the blows.
Oh for a man to weld it then, in one trip-hammer strain,
Till even first-class passengers could tell the meanin' plain!

But no one cares except mysel' that serve an' understand
My seven thousand horse-power here. Eh, Lord! They're grand –
                                    they're grand!
Uplift am I? When first in store the new-made beasties stood,
Were Ye cast down that breathed the Word declarin' all things
                                           good?
Not so! O' that warld-liftin' joy no after-fall could vex,
Ye've left a glimmer still to cheer the Man – the Arrtifex!
*That* holds, in spite o' knock and scale, o' friction, waste an' slip,
An' by that light – now, mark my word – we'll build the Perfect
                                           Ship.
I'll never last to judge her lines or take her curve – not I.
But I ha' lived an' I ha' worked. Be thanks to Thee, Most High!
An' I ha' done what I ha' done – judge Thou if ill or well –
Always Thy Grace preventin' me ...
                           Losh! Yon's the 'Stand-by' bell.
Pilot so soon? His flare it is. The mornin'-watch is set.
Well, God be thanked, as I was sayin', I'm no Pelagian yet.
Now I'll tak' on ...
    'Morrn, Ferguson. *Man, have ye ever thought*
*What your good leddy costs in coal? ... I'll burn 'em down to port.*


# The Song of the Banjo
## 1894


You couldn't pack a Broadwood half a mile –
    You mustn't leave a fiddle in the damp –
You couldn't raft an organ up the Nile,
    And play it in an Equatorial swamp.
*I* travel with the cooking-pots and pails –
    I'm sandwiched 'tween the coffee and the pork –
And when the dusty column checks and tails,
    You should hear me spur the rearguard to a walk!

With my '*Pilly-willy-winky-winky-popp!*'
  (Oh, it's any tune that comes into my head!)
So I keep 'em moving forward till they drop;
  So I play 'em up to water and to bed.

In the silence of the camp before the fight,
  When it's good to make your will and say your prayer,
You can hear my *strumpty-tumpty* overnight,
  Explaining ten to one was always fair.
I'm the Prophet of the Utterly Absurd,
  Of the Patently Impossible and Vain –
And when the Thing that Couldn't has occurred,
  Give me time to change my leg and go again.

    With my '*Tumpa-tumpa-tumpa-tumpa-tump!*'
      In the desert where the dung-fed camp-smoke curled.
    There was never voice before us till I fed our lonely chorus,
      I – the war-drum of the White Man round the world!

By the bitter road the Younger Son must tread,
  Ere he win to hearth and saddle of his own –
'Mid the riot of the shearers at the shed,
  In the silence of the herder's hut alone –
In the twilight, on a bucket upside down,
  Hear me babble what the weakest won't confess –
I am Memory and Torment – I am Town!
  I am all that ever went with evening dress!

    With my '*Tunka-tunka-tunka-tunka-tunk!*'
      (So the lights – the London Lights – grow near and plain!)
    So I rowel 'em afresh towards the Devil and the Flesh,
      Till I bring my broken rankers home again.

In desire of many marvels over sea,
  Where the new-raised tropic city sweats and roars,
I have sailed with Young Ulysses from the quay
  Till the anchor rumbled down on stranger shores.
He is blooded to the open and the sky,
  He is taken in a snare that shall not fail,
He shall hear me singing strongly, till he die,
  Like the shouting of a backstay in a gale.

With my 'Hya! Heeya! Heeya! Hullah! Haul!'
  (Oh, the green that thunders aft along the deck!)
Are you sick o' towns and men? You must sign and sail again,
  For it's 'Johnny Bowlegs, pack your kit and trek!'

Through the gorge that gives the stars at noon-day clear –
  Up the pass that packs the scud beneath our wheel –
Round the bluff that sinks her thousand fathom sheer –
  Down the valley with our guttering brakes asqueal:
Where the trestle groans and quivers in the snow,
  Where the many-shedded levels loop and twine,
Hear me lead my reckless children from below
  Till we sing the Song of Roland to the pine!

    With my 'Tinka-tinka-tinka-tinka-tink!'
      (Oh, the axe has cleared the mountain, croup and crest!)
    And we ride the iron stallions down to drink,
      Through the cañons to the waters of the West!

And the tunes that mean so much to you alone –
  Common tunes that make you choke and blow your nose –
Vulgar tunes that bring the laugh that brings the groan –
  I can rip your very heartstrings out with those;
With the feasting, and the folly, and the fun –
  And the lying, and the lusting, and the drink,
And the merry play that drops you, when you're done.
  To the thoughts that burn like irons if you think.

    With my 'Plunka-lunka-lunka-lunka-lunk!'
      Here's a trifle on account of pleasure past,
    Ere the wit that made you win gives you eyes to see your sin
      And – the heavier repentance at the last!

Let the organ moan her sorrow to the roof –
  I have told the naked stars the Grief of Man!
Let the trumpet snare the foeman to the proof –
  I have known Defeat, and mocked it as we ran!
My bray ye may not alter nor mistake
  When I stand to jeer the fatted Soul of Things,
But the Song of Lost Endeavour that I make,
  Is it hidden in the twanging of the strings?

With my '*Ta-ra-rara-rara-ra-ra-rrrp!*'
    (Is it naught to you that hear and pass me by?)
But the word – the word is mine, when the order moves the
                                          line
    And the lean, locked ranks go roaring down to die!

The grandam of my grandam was the Lyre –
    (Oh, the blue below the little fisher-huts!)
That the Stealer stooping beachward filled with fire,
    Till she bore my iron head and ringing guts!
By the wisdom of the centuries I speak –
    To the tune of yestermorn I set the truth –
I, the joy of life unquestioned –  I, the Greek –
    I, the everlasting Wonder-song of Youth!

    With my '*Tinka-tinka-tinka-tinka-tink!*'
        (What d'ye lack, my noble masters! What d'ye lack?)
     So I draw the world together link by link:
        Yea, from Delos up to Limerick and back!


# The Three-Decker

## 1894

*('The three-volume novel is extinct.')*


Full thirty foot she towered from waterline to rail.
It took a watch to steer her, and a week to shorten sail;
But, spite of all modern notions, I've found her first and best –
The only certain packet for the Islands of the Blest.

Fair held the breeze behind us – 'twas warm with lovers' prayers.
We'd stolen wills for ballast and a crew of missing heirs.
They shipped as Able Bastards till the Wicked Nurse confessed,
And they worked the old three-decker to the Islands of the Blest.

By ways no gaze could follow, a course unspoiled of Cook,
Per Fancy, fleetest in man, our titled berths we took,
With maids of matchless beauty and parentage unguessed,
And a Church of England parson for the Islands of the Blest.

We asked no social questions – we pumped no hidden shame –
We never talked obstetrics when the Little Stranger came:
We left the Lord in Heaven, we left the fiends in Hell.
We weren't exactly Yussufs, but – Zuleika didn't tell.

No moral doubt assailed us, so when the port we neared,
The villain had his flogging at the gangway, and we cheered.
'Twas fiddle in the foc's'le – 'twas garlands on the mast,
For every one got married, and I went ashore at last.

I left 'em all in couples a-kissing on the decks.
I left the lovers loving and the parents writing cheques.
In endless English comfort, by country-folk caressed,
I left the old three-decker at the Islands of the Blest! ...

That route is barred to steamers: you'll never lift again
Our purple-painted headlands or the lordly keeps of Spain.
They're just beyond your skyline, howe'er so far you cruise
In a ram-you-damn-you liner with a brace of bucking screws.

Swing round your aching searchlight – 'twill show no haven's
                                                    peace.
Ay, blow your shrieking sirens at the deaf, grey-headed seas!
Boom out the dripping oil-bags to skin the deep's unrest –
And you aren't one knot nearer to the Islands of the Blest.

But when you're threshing, crippled, with broken bridge and rail,
At a drogue of dead convictions to hold your head to gale,
Calm as the Flying Dutchman, from truck to taffrail dressed,
You'll see the old three-decker for the Islands of the Blest.

You'll see her tiering canvas in sheeted silver spread,
You'll hear the long-drawn thunder 'neath her leaping
                                                    figure-head;
While far, so far above you, her tall poop-lanterns shine
Unvexed by wind or weather like the candles round a shrine!

Hull down – hull down and under – she dwindles to a speck,
With noise of pleasant music and dancing on the deck.
All's well – all's well aboard her – she's left you far behind,
With a scent of old-world roses through the fog that ties you blind.

Her crews are babes or madmen? Her port is all to make?
You're manned by Truth and Science, and you steam for
steaming's sake?
Well, tinker up your engines – you know your business best –
*She*'s taking tired people to the Islands of the Blest!

# In the Neolithic Age
## 1895

In the Neolithic Age savage warfare did I wage
For food and fame and woolly horses' pelt.
I was singer to my clan in that dim, red Dawn of Man,
And I sang of all we fought and feared and felt.

Yea, I sang as now I sing, when the Prehistoric spring
Made the piled Biscayan ice-pack split and shove;
And the troll and gnome and dwerg, and the Gods of Cliff and
Berg
Were about me and beneath me and above.

But a rival, of Solutré, told the tribe my style was *outré* –
'Neath a tomahawk, of diorite, he fell.
And I left my views on Art, barbed and tanged, below the heart
Of a mammothistic etcher at Grenelle.

Then I stripped them, scalp from skull, and my hunting-dogs fed
full,
And their teeth I threaded neatly on a thong;
And I wiped my mouth and said, 'It is well that they are dead,
For I know my work is right and theirs was wrong.'

But my Totem saw the shame; from his ridgepole-shrine he came,
    And he told me in a vision of the night: –
'There are nine and sixty ways of constructing tribal lays,
    And every single one of them is right!'

*

Then the silence closed upon me till They put new clothing on me
    Of whiter, weaker flesh and bone more frail;  .
And I stepped beneath Time's finger, once again a tribal singer,
    And a minor poet certified by Traill!

Still they skirmish to and fro, men my messmates on the snow,
    When we headed off the aurochs turn for turn;
When the rich Allobrogenses never kept amanuenses,
    And our only plots were piled in lakes at Berne.

Still a cultured Christian age sees us scuffle, squeak, and rage,
    Still we pinch and slap and jabber, scratch and dirk;
Still we let our business slide – as we dropped the half-dressed
                                  hide –
    To show a fellow-savage how to work.

Still the world is wondrous large – seven seas from marge to
                                   marge –
    And it holds a vast of various kinds of man;
And the wildest dreams of Kew are the facts of Khatmandhu
    And the crimes of Clapham chaste in Martaban.

Here's my wisdom for your use, as I learned it when the moose
    And the reindeer roamed where Paris roars to-night: –
'There are nine and sixty ways of constructing tribal lays,
    And–every–single–one–of–them–is–right!'

# 'When 'Omer Smote 'Is Bloomin' Lyre'

*(Introduction to the Barrack-Room Ballads in* The Seven Seas)

When 'Omer smote 'is bloomin' lyre,
   He'd 'eard men sing by land an' sea;
An' what he thought 'e might require,
   'E went an' took – the same as me!

The market-girls an' fishermen,
   The shepherds an' the sailors, too,
They 'eard old songs turn up again,
   But kep' it quiet – same as you!

They knew 'e stole; 'e knew they knowed.
   They didn't tell, nor make a fuss,
But winked at 'Omer down the road,
   An' 'e winked back – the same as us!


# 'For To Admire'

The Injian Ocean sets an' smiles
   So sof', so bright, so bloomin' blue;
There aren't a wave for miles an' miles
   Excep' the jiggle from the screw.
The ship is swep', the day is done,
   The bugle's gone for smoke and play;
An' black ag'in the settin' sun
   The Lascar sings, '*Hum deckty hai!*'

*For to admire an' for to see,*
   *For to be'old this world so wide –*
*It never done no good to me,*
   *But I can't drop it if I tried!*

I see the sergeants pitchin' quoits,
    I 'ear the women laugh an' talk,
I spy upon the quarter-deck
    The orficers an' lydies walk.
I thinks about the things that was,
    An' leans an' looks acrost the sea,
Till, spite of all the crowded ship
    There's no one lef' alive but me.

The things that was which I 'ave seen,
    In barrick, camp, an' action too,
I tells them over by myself,
    An' sometimes wonders if they're true;
For they was odd – most awful odd –
    But all the same, now they are o'er,
There must be 'eaps o' plenty such,
    An' if I wait I'll see some more.

Oh, I 'ave come upon the books,
    An' frequent broke a barrick-rule,
An' stood beside an' watched myself
    Be'avin' like a bloomin' fool.
I paid my price for findin' out,
    Nor never grutched the price I paid,
But sat in Clink without my boots,
    Admirin' 'ow the world was made.

Be'old a cloud upon the beam,
    An' 'umped above the sea appears
Old Aden, like a barrick-stove
    That no one's lit for years an' years!
I passed by that when I began,
    An' I go 'ome the road I came,
A time-expired soldier-man
    With six years' service to 'is name.

My girl she said, 'Oh, stay with me!'
    My mother 'eld me to 'er breast.
They've never written none, an' so
    They must 'ave gone with all the rest –
With all the rest which I 'ave seen
    An' found an' known an' met along.
I cannot say the things I feel,
    And so I sing my evenin' song:

*For to admire an' for to see,*
    *For to be'old this world so wide –*
*It never done no good to me,*
    *But I can't drop it if I tried!*


## Sestina of the Tramp-Royal
### 1896


Speakin' in general, I 'ave tried 'em all –
The 'appy roads that take you o'er the world.
Speakin' in general, I 'ave found them good
For such as cannot use one bed too long,
But must get 'ence, the same as I 'ave done,
An' go observin' matters till they die.

What do it matter where or 'ow we die,
So long as we've our 'ealth to watch it all –
The different ways that different things are done.
An' men an' women lovin' in this world;
Takin' our chances as they come along,
An' when they ain't, pretendin' they are good?

In cash or credit – no, it aren't no good;
You 'ave to 'ave the 'abit or you'd die,
Unless you lived your life but one day long,
Nor didn't prophesy not fret at all,
But drew your tucker some'ow from the world,
An' never bothered what you might ha' done.

But, Gawd, what things are they I 'aven't done?
I've turned my 'and to most, an' turned it good,
In various situations round the world –
For 'im that doth not work must surely die;
But that's no reason man should labour all
'Is life on one same shift – life's none so long.

Therefore, from job to job I've moved along.
Pay couldn't 'old me when my time was done,
For something in my 'ead upset it all,
Till I 'ad dropped whatever 'twas for good,
An', out at sea, be'eld the dock-lights die,
An' met my mate – the wind that tramps the world!

It's like a book, I think, this bloomin' world,
Which you can read and care for just so long,
But presently you feel that you will die
Unless you get the page you're readin' done,
An' turn another – likely not so good;
But what you're after is to turn 'em all.

Gawd bless this world! Whatever she 'ath done –
Excep' when awful long – I've found it good.
So write, before I die, "'E liked it all!'

# Recessional

## 1897

God of our fathers, known of old –
    Lord of our far-flung battle-line,
Beneath whose awful hand we hold
    Dominion over palm and pine –
Lord God of Hosts, be with us yet,
Lest we forget – lest we forget!

The tumult and the shouting dies;
    The Captains and the Kings depart:
Still stands Thine ancient sacrifice,
    An humble and a contrite heart.
Lord God of Hosts, be with us yet,
Lest we forget – lest we forget!

Far-called, our navies melt away;
    On dune and headland sinks the fire:
Lo, all our pomp of yesterday
    Is one with Nineveh and Tyre!
Judge of the Nations, spare us yet,
Lest we forget – lest we forget!

If, drunk with sight of power, we loose
    Wild tongues that have not Thee in awe,
Such boastings as the Gentiles use,
    Or lesser breeds without the Law –
Lord God of Hosts, be with us yet,
Lest we forget – lest we forget!

For heathen heart that puts her trust
    In reeking tube and iron shard,
All valiant dust that builds on dust,
    And guarding, calls not Thee to guard,
For frantic boast and foolish word –
Thy Mercy on Thy People, Lord!

# from *Verses on Games*

(*To* An Almanac of Twelve Sports, *by W. Nicholson, 1898*)

### JANUARY
### (*Hunting*)

Certes, it is a noble sport,
   And men have quitted selle and swum for't.
But I am of the meeker sort
   And I prefer Surtees in comfort.

Reach me my *Handley Cross* again,
   My run, where never danger lurks, is
With Jorrocks and his deathless train –
   Pigg, Binjimin, and Artaxerxes.

### JUNE
### (*Cricket*)

Thank God who made the British Isles
   And taught me how to play;
I do not worship crocodiles,
   Or bow the knee to clay!
Give me a willow wand and I
   With hide and cork and twine
From century to century
   Will gambol round my shrine!

### AUGUST
### (*Coaching*)

The Pious Horse to church may trot,
   A maid may work a man's salvation ...
Four horses and a girl are not
   However, roads to reformation.

### SEPTEMBER
(*Shooting*)

'Peace upon Earth, Goodwill to men'
   So greet we Christmas Day!
Oh, Christian, load your gun and then,
   Oh, Christian, out and slay.


### OCTOBER
(*Golf*)

Why Golf is Art and Art is Golf
   We have not far to seek –
So much depends upon the lie,
   So much upon the cleek.


### DECEMBER
(*Skating*)

Over the ice she flies
   Perfect and poised and fair.
Stars in my true-love's eyes
   Teach me to do and dare.
Now will I fly as she flies –
   Woe for the stars that misled.
Stars I beheld in her eyes
   Now do I see in my head.

# The White Man's Burden
## *1899*

*(The United States and the Philippine Islands)*

Take up the White Man's burden –
  Send forth the best ye breed –
Go bind your sons to exile
  To serve your captives' need;
To wait in heavy harness
  On fluttered folk and wild –
Your new-caught, sullen peoples,
  Half devil and half child.

Take up the White Man's burden –
  In patience to abide,
To veil the threat of terror
  And check the show of pride;
By open speech and simple,
  An hundred times made plain,
To seek another's profit,
  And work another's gain.

Take up the White Man's burden –
  The savage wars of peace –
Fill full the mouth of Famine
  And bid the sickness cease;
And when your goal is nearest
  The end for others sought,
Watch Sloth and heathen Folly
  Bring all your hope to nought.

Take up the White Man's burden –
  No tawdry rule of kings,
But toil of serf and sweeper –
  The tale of common things.
The ports ye shall not enter,
  The roads ye shall not tread,
Go make them with your living,
  And mark them with your dead!

Take up the White Man's burden –
    And reap his old reward:
The blame of those ye better,
    The hate of those ye guard –
The cry of hosts ye humour
    (Ah, slowly!) toward the light: –
'Why brought ye us from bondage,
    Our loved Egyptian night?'

Take up the White Man's burden –
    Ye dare not stoop to less –
Nor call too loud on Freedom
    To cloak your weariness;
By all ye cry or whisper,
    By all ye leave or do,
The silent, sullen peoples
    Shall weigh your Gods and you.

Take up the White Man's burden –
    Have done with childish days –
The lightly proffered laurel,
    The easy, ungrudged praise.
Comes now, to search your manhood
    Through all the thankless years,
Cold-edged with dear-bought wisdom,
    The judgment of your peers!

# The Absent-Minded Beggar

When you've shouted 'Rule Britannia', when you've sung 'God
save the Queen',
   When you've finished killing Kruger with your mouth,
Will you kindly drop a shilling in my little tambourine
   For a gentleman in khaki ordered South?
He's an absent-minded beggar, and his weaknesses are great –
   But we and Paul must take him as we find him –
He is out on active service, wiping something off a slate –
   And he's left a lot of little things behind him!
Duke's son – cook's son – son of a hundred kings –
   (Fifty thousand horse and foot going to Table Bay!)
Each of 'em doing his country's work
   (and who's to look after their things?)
Pass the hat for your credit's sake,
               and pay – pay – pay !

There are girls he married secret, asking no permission to,
   For he knew he wouldn't get it if he did.
There is gas and coals and vittles, and the house-rent falling due,
   And it's more than rather likely there's a kid.
There are girls he walked with casual. They'll be sorry now he's
gone,
   For an absent-minded beggar they will find him,
But it ain't the time for sermons with the winter coming on
   We must help the girl that Tommy's left behind him!
Cook's son – Duke's son – son of a belted Earl
   Son of a Lambeth publican – it's all the same to-day !
Each of 'em doing his country's work
   (and who's to look after the girl?)
Pass the hat for your credit's sake,
               and pay – pay – pay !

There are families by thousands, far too proud to beg or speak,
    And they'll put their sticks and bedding up the spout,
And they'll live on half o' nothing, paid 'em punctual once a
                                                    week,
    'Cause the man that earns the wage is ordered out.
He's an absent-minded beggar, but he heard his country call,
    And his reg'ment didn't need to send to find him!
He chucked his job and joined it – so the job before us all
    Is to help the home that Tommy's left behind him!
Duke's job – cook's job – gardener, baronet, groom,
    Mews or palace or paper-shop, there's someone gone away!
Each of 'em doing his country's work
    (and who's to look after the room?)
Pass the hat for your credit's sake,
                        and pay – pay – pay !

Let us manage so as, later, we can look him in the face,
    And tell him – what he'd very much prefer –
That, while he saved the Empire, his employer saved his place,
    And his mates (that's you and me) looked out for *her*.
He's an absent-minded beggar and he may forget it all,
    But we do not want his kiddies to remind him
That we sent 'em to the workhouse while their daddy
                                        hammered Paul,
    So we'll help the homes that Tommy left behind him!
Cook's home – Duke's home – home of a millionaire,
    (Fifty thousand horse and foot going to Table Bay!)
Each of 'em doing his country's work
    (and what have you got to spare?)
Pass the hat for your credit's sake,
                        and pay – pay – pay !

# The Islanders
## 1902

*No doubt but ye are the People – your throne is above the King's.*
*Whoso speaks in your presence must say acceptable things:*
*Bowing the head in worship, bending the knee in fear –*
*Bringing the word well smoothen – such as a King should hear.*


Fenced by your careful fathers, ringed by your leaden seas,
Long did ye wake in quiet and long lie down at ease;
Till ye said of Strife 'What is it?', of the Sword 'It is far from our
                                                        ken';
Till ye made a sport of your shrunken hosts and a toy of your
                                                    armèd men.
Ye stopped your ears to the warning – ye would neither look nor
                                                        heed –
Ye set our leisure before their toil and your lusts above their need.
Because of your witless learning and your beasts of warren and
                                                        chase,
Ye grudged your sons to their service and your fields for their
                                                    camping-place.
Ye forced them glean in the highways the straw for the bricks
                                                    they brought;
Ye forced them follow in byways the craft that ye never taught.
Ye hampered and hindered and crippled; ye thrust out of sight
                                                    and away
Those that would serve you for honour and those that served
                                                    you for pay.
Then were the judgments loosened; then was your shame revealed,
At the hands of a little people, few but apt in the field.
Yet ye were saved by a remnant (and your land's long-suffering
                                                        star),
When your strong men cheered in their millions while your
                                                striplings went to the war.
Sons of the sheltered city – unmade, unhandled, unmeet –
Ye pushed them raw to the battle as ye picked them raw from
                                                    the street.
And what did ye look they should compass? Warcraft learned in
                                                    a breath,

84

Knowledge unto occasion at the first far view of Death?
So? And ye train your horses and the dogs ye feed and prize?
How are the beasts more worthy than the souls, your sacrifice?
But ye said 'Their valour shall show them'; but ye said 'The end
is close.'
And ye sent them comfits and pictures to help them harry your
foes:
And ye vaunted your fathomless power, and ye flaunted your
iron pride,
Ere – ye fawned on the Younger Nations for the men who could
shoot and ride!
Then ye returned to your trinkets; then ye contented your souls
With the flannelled fools at the wicket or the muddied oafs at
the goals.

Given to strong delusion, wholly believing a lie,
Ye saw that the land lay fenceless, and ye let the months go by
Waiting some easy wonder, hoping some saving sign –
Idle – openly idle – in the lee of the forespent Line.
Idle – except for your boasting – and what is your boasting worth
If ye grudge a year of service to the lordliest life on earth?
Ancient, effortless, ordered, cycle on cycle set,
Life so long untroubled, that ye who inherit forget
It was not made with the mountains, it is not one with the deep.
Men, not gods, devised it. Men, not gods, must keep.
Men, not children, servants, or kinsfolk called from afar,
But each man born in the Island broke to the matter of war.
Soberly and by custom taken and trained for the same,
Each man born in the Island entered at youth to the game –
As it were almost cricket, not to be mastered in haste,
But after trial and labour, by temperance, living chaste.
As it were almost cricket – as it were even your play,
Weighed and pondered and worshipped, and practised day and
day.

So ye shall bide sure-guarded when the restless lightnings wake
In the womb of the blotting war-cloud, and the pallid nations
quake.

So, at the haggard trumpets, instant your soul shall leap
Forthright, accoutred, accepting – alert from the wells of sleep.
So at the threat ye shall summon – so at the need ye shall send
Men, not children or servants, tempered and taught to the end;
Cleansed of servile panic, slow to dread or despise,

Humble because of knowledge, mighty by sacrifice ...
But ye say 'It will mar our comfort.' Ye say 'It will minish our
trade.'
Do ye wait for the spattered shrapnel ere ye learn how a gun is
laid?
For the low, red glare to southward when the raided coast-
towns burn?
(Light ye shall have on that lesson, but little time to learn.)
Will ye pitch some white pavilion, and lustily even the odds,
With nets and hoops and mallets, with rackets and bats and rods?
Will the rabbit war with your foemen – the red deer horn them
for hire?
Your kept cock-pheasant keep you? – he is master of many a shire.
Arid, aloof, incurious, unthinking, unthanking, gelt,
Will ye loose your schools to flout them till their brow-beat
columns melt?
Will ye pray them or preach them, or print them, or ballot them
back from your shore?
Will your workmen issue a mandate to bid them strike no more?
Will ye rise and dethrone your rulers? (Because ye were idle both?
Pride by Insolence chastened? Indolence purged by Sloth?)
No doubt but ye are the People; who shall make you afraid?
Also your gods are many; no doubt but your gods shall aid.
Idols of greasy altars built for the body's ease;
Proud little brazen Baals and talking fetishes;
Teraphs of sept and party and wise wood-pavement gods –
*These* shall come down to the battle and snatch you from under
the rods?
From the gusty, flickering gun-roll with viewless salvoes rent,
And the pitted hail of the bullets that tell not whence they were
sent.
When ye are ringed as with iron, when ye are scourged as with
whips,
When the meat is yet in your belly, and the boast is yet on your
lips;
When ye go forth at morning and the noon beholds you broke,
Ere ye lie down at even, your remnant, under the yoke?

*No doubt but ye are the People – absolute, strong, and wise;*
*Whatever your heart has desired ye have not withheld from your eyes.*
*On your own heads, in your own hands, the sin and the saving lies!*

# from *Just So Verses*

## *'The Camel's hump is an ugly lump'*

The Camel's hump is an ugly lump
    Which well you may see at the Zoo;
But uglier yet is the hump we get
    From having too little to do.

Kiddies and grown-ups too-oo-oo,
If we haven't enough to do-oo-oo,
        We get the hump –
        Cameelious hump –
The hump that is black and blue!

We climb out of bed with a frouzly head,
    And a snarly-yarly voice.
We shiver and scowl and we grunt and we growl
    At our bath and our boots and our toys;

And there ought to be a corner for me
(And I know there is one for you)
        When we get the hump –
        Cameelious hump –
The hump that is black and blue!

The cure for this ill is not to sit still,
    Or frowst with a book by the fire;
But to take a large hoe and a shovel also,
    And dig till you gently perspire;

And then you will find that the sun and the wind,
And the Djinn of the Garden too,
        Have lifted the hump –
        The horrible hump –
The hump that is black and blue!

I get it as well as you-oo-oo –
If I haven't enough to do-oo-oo!
We all get hump –
Cameelious hump –
Kiddies and grown-ups too!


## 'I keep six honest serving-men'

I keep six honest serving-men
    (They taught me all I knew);
Their names are What and Why and When
    And How and Where and Who.
I send them over land and sea,
    I send them east and west;
But after they have worked for me,
    *I* give them all a rest.

*I* let them rest from nine till five,
    For I am busy then,
As well as breakfast, lunch, and tea,
    For they are hungry men:
But different folk have different views;
    I know a person small –
She keeps ten million serving-men,
    Who get no rest at all!

She sends 'em abroad on her own affairs,
    From the second she opens her eyes –
One million Hows, two million Wheres,
    And seven million Whys!


## Merrow Down

### I

There runs a road by Merrow Down –
    A grassy track to-day it is –
An hour out of Guildford town,
    Above the river Wey it is.

Here, when they heard the horse-bells ring,
    The ancient Britons dressed and rode
To watch the dark Phoenicians bring
    Their goods along the Western Road.

And, here, or hereabouts, they met
    To hold their racial talks and such –
To barter beads for Whitby jet,
    And tin for gay shell torques and such.

But long and long before that time
    (When bison used to roam on it)
Did Taffy and her Daddy climb
    That Down, and had their home on it.

Then beavers built in Broadstonebrook
    And made a swamp where Bramley stands;
And bears from Shere would come and look
    For Taffimai where Shamley stands.

The Wey, that Taffy called Wagai,
    Was more than six times bigger then;
And all the Tribe of Tegumai
    They cut a noble figure then!


II

Of all the Tribe of Tegumai
    Who cut that figure, none remain –
On Merrow Down the cuckoos cry –
    The silence and the sun remain.

But as the faithful years return
    And hearts unwounded sing again,
Comes Taffy dancing through the fern
    To lead the Surrey spring again.

Her brows are bound with bracken-fronds,
    And golden elf-locks fly above;
Her eyes are bright as diamonds
    And bluer than the sky above.

In moccasins and deer-skin cloak,
    Unfearing, free and fair she flits,
And lights her little damp-wood smoke
    To show her Daddy where she flits.

For far – oh, very far behind,
    So far she cannot call to him,
Comes Tegumai alone to find
    The daughter that was all to him!


## Lichtenberg

*(New South Wales Contingent)*


Smells are surer than sounds or sights
    To make your heart-strings crack –
They start those awful voices o' nights
    That whisper, 'Old man, come back!'
That must be why the big things pass
    And the little things remain,
Like the smell of the wattle by Lichtenberg,
    Riding in, in the rain.

There was some silly fire on the flank
    And the small wet drizzling down –
There were the sold-out shops and the bank
    And the wet, wide-open town;
*And* we were doing escort-duty
    To somebody's baggage-train,
And I smelt wattle by Lichtenberg –
    Riding in, in the rain.

It was all Australia to me –
  All I had found or missed:
Every face I was crazy to see,
  And every woman I'd kissed:
All that I shouldn't ha' done, God knows!
  (As He knows I'll do it again),
That smell of the wattle round Lichtenberg,
  Riding in, in the rain!

And I saw Sydney the same as ever,
  The picnics and brass-bands;
And my little homestead on Hunter River
  And my new vines joining hands.
It all came over me in one act
  Quick as a shot through the brain –
With the smell of the wattle round Lichtenberg,
  Riding in, in the rain.

I have forgotten a hundred fights,
  But one I shall not forget –
With the raindrops bunging up my sights
  And my eyes bunged up with wet;
And through the crack and the stink of the cordite
  (Ah Christ! My country again!)
The smell of the wattle by Lichtenberg,
  Riding in, in the rain!

# The Return of the Children

('*"They"*' – Traffics and Discoveries)

Neither the harps nor the crowns amused, nor the cherubs'
dove-winged races –
Holding hands forlornly the Children wandered beneath the
Dome,
Plucking the splendid robes of the passers-by, and with pitiful
faces
Begging what Princes and Powers refused: – 'Ah, please will you
let us go home?'

Over the jewelled floor, nigh weeping, ran to them Mary the
Mother,
Kneeled and caressed and made promise with kisses, and drew
them along to the gateway –
Yea, the all-iron unbribeable Door which Peter must guard and
none other.
Straightway She took the Keys from his keeping, and opened
and freed them straightway.

Then, to Her Son, Who had seen and smiled, She said: 'On the
night that I bore Thee,
What didst Thou care for a love beyond mine or a heaven that
was not my arm?
Didst Thou push from the nipple, O Child, to hear the angels
adore Thee
When we two lay in the breath of the kine?' And He said: –
'Thou hast done no harm.'

So through the Void the Children ran homeward merrily hand
in hand,
Looking neither to left nor right where the breathless Heavens
stood still.
And the Guards of the Void resheathed their swords, for they
heard the Command:
'Shall I that have suffered the Children to come to Me hold them
against their will?'

# Harp Song of the Dane Women

*('The Knights of the Joyous Venture' – Puck of Pook's Hill)*

What is a woman that you forsake her,
And the hearth-fire and the home-acre,
To go with the old grey Widow-maker?

She has no house to lay a guest in –
But one chill bed for all to rest in,
That the pale suns and the stray bergs nest in.

She has no strong white arms to fold you,
But the ten-times-fingering weed  to hold you –
Out on the rocks where the tide has rolled you.

Yet, when the signs of summer thicken,
And the ice breaks, and the birch-buds quicken,
Yearly you turn from our side, and sicken –

Sicken again for the shouts and the slaughters.
You steal away to the lapping waters,
And look at your ship in her winter-quarters.

You forget our mirth, and talk at the tables,
The kine in the shed and the horse in the stables –
To pitch her sides and go over her cables.

Then you drive out where the storm-clouds swallow,
And the sound of your oar-blades, falling hollow,
Is all we have left through the months to follow.

Ah, what is Woman that you forsake her,
And the hearth-fire and the home-acre,
To go with the old grey Widow-maker?

# 'Cities and Thrones and Powers'

*( 'A Centurion of the Thirtieth' – Puck of Pook's Hill)*

Cities and Thrones and Powers
   Stand in Time's eye,
Almost as long as flowers,
   Which daily die:
But, as new buds put forth
   To glad new men,
Out of the spent and unconsidered Earth
   The Cities rise again.

This season's Daffodil,
   She never hears
What change, what chance, what chill,
   Cut down last year's;
But with bold countenance,
   And knowledge small,
Esteems her seven days' continuance,
   To be perpetual.

So Time that is o'er-kind
   To all that be,
Ordains us e'en as blind,
   As bold as she:
That in our very death,
   And burial sure,
Shadow to shadow, well persuaded, saith,
   'See how our works endure!'

# A Song to Mithras

## Hymn of the XXX Legion: circa A.D. 350

*('On the Great Wall'* – Puck of Pook's Hill)


Mithras, God of the Morning, our trumpets waken the Wall!
'Rome is above the Nations, but Thou art over all!'
Now as the names are answered, and the guards are marched
away,
Mithras, also a soldier, give us strength for the day!

Mithras, God of the Noontide, the heather swims in the heat,
Our helmets scorch our foreheads, our sandals burn our feet.
Now in the ungirt hour – now lest we blink and drowse,
Mithras, also a soldier, keep us true to our vows!

Mithras, God of the Sunset, low on the Western main –
Thou descending immortal, immortal to rise again!
Now when the watch is ended, now when the wine is drawn,
Mithras, also a soldier, keep us pure till the dawn!

Mithras, God of the Midnight, here where the great Bull dies,
Look on Thy children in darkness. Oh, take our sacrifice!
Many roads Thou hast fashioned – all of them lead to the Light!
Mithras, also a soldier, teach us to die aright!

# A Pict Song

('*The Winged Hats*' – Puck of Pook's Hill)


Rome never looks where she treads.
   Always her heavy hooves fall
On our stomachs, our hearts or our heads;
   And Rome never heeds when we bawl.
Her sentries pass on – that is all,
   And we gather behind them in hordes,
And plot to reconquer the Wall,
   With only our tongues for our swords.

We are the Little Folk – we!
   Too little to love or to hate.
Leave us alone and you'll see
   How we can drag down the Great!
We are the worm in the wood!
   We are the rot at the root!
We are the taint in the blood!
   We are the thorn in the foot!

Mistletoe killing an oak –
   Rats gnawing cables in two –
Moths making holes in a cloak –
   How they must love what they do!
Yes – and we Little Folk too,
   We are busy as they –
Working our works out of view –
   Watch, and you'll see it some day!

No indeed! We are not strong,
   But we know Peoples that are.
Yes, and we'll guide them along
   To smash and destroy you in War!
*We* shall be slaves just the same?
   Yes, we have always been slaves,
But you – you will die of the shame,
   And then we shall dance on your graves!

We are the Little Folk, we, etc.

# A Smuggler's Song

('*Hal o' the Draft*' – Puck of Pook's Hill)

If you wake at midnight, and hear a horse's feet,
Don't go drawing back the blind, or looking in the street.
Them that asks no questions isn't told a lie.
Watch the wall, my darling, while the Gentlemen go by!
      Five and twenty ponies,
      Trotting through the dark –
      Brandy for the Parson,
      'Baccy for the Clerk;
      Laces for a lady; letters for a spy,
And watch the wall, my darling, while the Gentlemen go by!

Running round the woodlump if you chance to find
Little barrels, roped and tarred, all full of brandy-wine,
Don't you shout to come and look, nor use 'em for your play.
Put the brishwood back again – and they'll be gone next day!

If you see the stable-door setting open wide;
If you see a tired horse lying down inside;
If your mother mends a coat cut about and tore;
If the lining's wet and warm – don't you ask no more!

If you meet King George's men, dressed in blue and red,
You be careful what you say, and mindful what is said.
If they call you 'pretty maid', and chuck you 'neath the chin,
Don't you tell where no one is, nor yet where no one's been!

Knocks and footsteps round the house – whistles after dark –
You've no call for running out till the house-dogs bark.
*Trusty*'s here, and *Pincher*'s here, and see how dumb they lie –
*They* don't fret to follow when the Gentlemen go by!

If you do as you've been told, 'likely there's a chance,
You'll be give a dainty doll, all the way from France,
With a cap of Valenciennes, and a velvet hood –
A present from the Gentlemen, along o' being good!
     Five and twenty ponies,
     Trotting through the dark –
     Brandy for the Parson,
     'Baccy for the Clerk.
Them that asks no questions isn't told a lie –
Watch the wall, my darling, while the Gentlemen go by!

# The Sons of Martha
## 1907

The Sons of Mary seldom bother, for they have inherited that
     good part;
But the Sons of Martha favour their Mother of the careful soul
     and the troubled heart.
And because she lost her temper once, and because she was rude
     to the Lord her Guest,
Her Sons must wait upon Mary's Sons, world without end,
     reprieve, or rest.

It is their care in all the ages to take the buffet and cushion the
     shock.
It is their care that the gear engages; it is their care that the
     switches lock.
It is their care that the wheels run truly; it is their care to embark
     and entrain,
Tally, transport, and deliver duly the Sons of Mary by land and
     main.

They say to mountains 'Be ye removed.' They say to the lesser
floods 'Be dry.'
Under their rods are the rocks reproved – they are not afraid of
that which is high.
Then do the hill-tops shake to the summit – then is the bed of the
deep laid bare,
That the Sons of Mary may overcome it, pleasantly sleeping and
unaware.

They finger death at their gloves' end where they piece and
repiece the living wires.
He rears against the gates they tend: they feed him hungry
behind their fires.
Early at dawn, ere men see clear, they stumble into his terrible stall,
And hale him forth like a haltered steer, and goad and turn him
till evenfall.

To these from birth is Belief forbidden; from these till death is
Relief afar.
They are concerned with matters hidden – under the earth-line
their altars are –
The secret fountains to follow up, waters withdrawn to restore
to the mouth,
And gather the floods as in a cup, and pour them again at a
city's drouth.

They do not preach that their God will rouse them a little before
the nuts work loose.
They do not teach that His Pity allows them to drop their job
when they dam'-well choose.
As in the thronged and the lighted ways, so in the dark and the
desert they stand,
Wary and watchful all their days that their brethren's days may
be long in the land.

Raise ye the stone or cleave the wood to make a path more fair
or flat –
Lo, it is black already with blood some Son of Martha spilled for
that!
Not as a ladder from earth to Heaven, not as a witness to any creed,
But simple service simply given to his own kind in their
common need.

99

And the Sons of Mary smile and are blessed – they know the
                                    Angels are on their side.
They know in them is the Grace confessed, and for them are the
                                    Mercies multiplied.
They sit at the Feet – they hear the Word – they see how truly
                                    the Promise runs.
They have cast their burden upon the Lord, and – the Lord He
                                    lays it on Martha's Sons!


# The Looking-Glass

('*Gloriana*' – Rewards and Fairies)


*Queen Bess was Harry's daughter!*

The Queen was in her chamber, and she was middling old.
Her petticoat was satin and her stomacher was gold.
Backwards and forwards and sideways did she pass,
Making up her mind to face the cruel looking-glass.
  The cruel looking-glass that will never show a lass
  As comely or as kindly or as young as once she was!

The Queen was in her chamber, a-combing of her hair,
There came Queen Mary's spirit and it stood behind her chair,
Singing 'Backwards and forwards and sideways may you pass,
But I will stand behind you till you face the looking-glass.
  The cruel looking-glass that will never show a lass
  As lovely or unlucky or as lonely as I was!'

The Queen was in her chamber, a-weeping very sore,
There came Lord Leicester's spirit and it scratched upon the door,
Singing 'Backwards and forwards and sideways may you pass,
But I will walk beside you till you face the looking-glass.
  The cruel looking-glass that will never show a lass,
  As hard and unforgiving or as wicked as you was!'

The Queen was in her chamber, her sins were on her head;
She looked the spirits up and down and statelily she said:
'Backwards and forwards and sideways though I've been,
Yet I am Harry's daughter and I am England's Queen!'
    And she faced the looking-glass (and whatever else there was),
    And she saw her day was over and she saw her beauty pass
    In the cruel looking-glass, that can always hurt a lass
    More hard than any ghost there is or any man there was!


## The Way Through the Woods

('*Marklake Witches*' – Rewards and Fairies)


They shut the road through the woods
Seventy years ago.
Weather and rain have undone it again,
And now you would never know
There was once a road through the woods
Before they planted the trees.
It is underneath the coppice and heath
And the thin anemones.
Only the keeper sees
That, where the ring-dove broods,
And the badgers roll at ease,
There was once a road through the woods.

Yet, if you enter the woods
Of a summer evening late,
When the night-air cools on the trout-ringed pools
Where the otter whistles his mate,
(They fear not men in the woods,
Because they see so few)
You will hear the beat of a horse's feet,
And the swish of a skirt in the dew,
Steadily cantering through
The misty solitudes,

As though they perfectly knew
The old lost road through the woods …
But there is no road through the woods.




# If –

('*Brother Square-Toes*' – Rewards and Fairies)


If you can keep your head when all about you
   Are losing theirs and blaming it on you,
If you can trust yourself when all men doubt you,
   But make allowance for their doubting too;
If you can wait and not be tired by waiting,
   Or being lied about, not deal in lies,
Or being hated, don't give way to hating,
   And yet don't look too good, nor talk too wise:

If you can dream – and not make dreams your master:
   If you can think – and not make thoughts your aim;
If you can meet with Triumph and Disaster
   And treat those two impostors just the same;
If you can bear to hear the truth you've spoken
   Twisted by knaves to make a trap for fools,
Or watch the things you gave your life to, broken,
   And stoop and build 'em up with worn-out tools:

If you can make one heap of all your winnings
   And risk it on one turn of pitch-and-toss,
And lose, and start again at your beginnings
   And never breathe a word about your loss;
If you can force your heart and nerve and sinew
   To serve your turn long after they are gone,
And so hold on when there is nothing in you
   Except the Will which says to them: 'Hold on!'

If you can talk with crowds and keep your virtue,
    Or walk with Kings – nor lose the common touch,
If neither foes nor loving friends can hurt you,
    If all men count with you, but none too much;
If you can fill the unforgiving minute
    With sixty minutes' worth of distance run,
Yours is the Earth and everything that's in it,
    And – which is more – you'll be a Man, my son!

# Eddi's Service

## (AD 687)

*('The Conversion of St Wilfrid' – Rewards and Fairies)*

Eddi, priest of St. Wilfrid
    In his chapel at Manhood End,
Ordered a midnight service
    For such as cared to attend.

But the Saxons were keeping Christmas,
    And the night was stormy as well.
Nobody came to service,
    Though Eddi rang the bell.

'Wicked weather for walking,'
    Said Eddi of Manhood End.
'But I must go on with the service
    For such as care to attend.'

The altar-lamps were lighted –
    An old marsh-donkey came,
Bold as a guest invited,
    And stared at the guttering flame.

The storm beat on at the windows,
    The water splashed on the floor,
And a wet, yoke-weary bullock
    Pushed in through the open door.

'How do I know what is greatest,
    How do I know what is least?
That is My Father's business,'
    Said Eddi, Wilfrid's priest.

'But – three are gathered together –
    Listen to me and attend.
I bring good news, my brethren!'
    Said Eddi of Manhood End.

And he told the Ox of a Manger
    And a Stall in Bethlehem,
And he spoke to the Ass of a Rider,
    That rode to Jerusalem.

They steamed and dripped in the chancel,
    They listened and never stirred,
While, just as though they were Bishops,
    Eddi preached them The Word,

Till the gale blew off on the marshes
    And the windows showed the day,
And the Ox and the Ass together
    Wheeled and clattered away.

And when the Saxons mocked him,
    Said Eddi of Manhood End,
'I dare not shut His chapel
    On such as care to attend.'

# The Female of the Species
## 1911

When the Himalayan peasant meets the he-bear in his pride,
He shouts to scare the monster, who will often turn aside.
But the she-bear thus accosted rends the peasant tooth and nail.
For the female of the species is more deadly than the male.

When Nag the basking cobra hears the careless foot of man,
He will sometimes wriggle sideways and avoid it if he can.
But his mate makes no such motion where she camps beside the
                                                       trail.
For the female of the species is more deadly than the male.

When the early Jesuit fathers preached to Hurons and Choctaws,
They prayed to be delivered from the vengeance of the squaws.
'Twas the women, not the warriors, turned those stark
                                        enthusiasts pale.
For the female of the species is more deadly than the male.

Man's timid heart is bursting with the things he must not say,
For the Woman that God gave him isn't his to give away;
But when hunter meets with husband, each confirms the other's
                                                       tale –

The female of the species is more deadly than the male.

Man, a bear in most relations – worm and savage otherwise –
Man propounds negotiations, Man accepts the compromise.
Very rarely will he squarely push the logic of a fact
To its ultimate conclusion in unmitigated act.

Fear, or foolishness, impels him, ere he lay the wicked low,
To concede some form of trial even to his fiercest foe.
Mirth obscene diverts his anger – Doubt and Pity oft perplex
Him in dealing with an issue – to the scandal of The Sex!

But the Woman that God gave him, every fibre of her frame
Proves her launched for one sole issue, armed and engined for
                                                   the same;
And to serve that single issue, lest the generations fail,
The female of the species must be deadlier than the male..

She who faces Death by torture for each life beneath her breast
May not deal in doubt or pity – must not swerve for fact or jest.
These be purely male diversions – not in these her honour dwells.
She the Other Law we live by, is that Law and nothing else.

She can bring no more to living than the powers that make her
great
As the Mother of the Infant and the Mistress of the Mate.
And when Babe and Man are lacking and she strides unclaimed
to claim
Her right as femme (and baron), her equipment is the same.

She is wedded to convictions – in default of grosser ties;
Her contentions are her children, Heaven help him who denies! –
He will meet no suave discussion, but the instant, white-hot, wild,
Wakened female of the species warring as for spouse and child.

Unprovoked and awful charges –  even so the she-bear fights,
Speech that drips, corrodes, and poisons – even so the cobra bites,
Scientific vivisection of one nerve till it is raw
And the victim writhes in anguish – like the Jesuit with the squaw!

So it comes that Man, the coward, when he gathers to confer
With his fellow-braves in council, dare not leave a place for her
Where, at war with Life and Conscience, he uplifts his erring
hands
To some God of Abstract Justice – which no woman understands.

And Man knows it! Knows, moreover, that the Woman that God
gave him
Must command but may not govern – shall enthral but not
enslave him.
And *She* knows, because She warns him, and Her instincts never
fail,
That the Female of Her Species is more deadly than the Male.

# Dane-geld

### (AD 980–1016)

It is always a temptation to an armed and agile nation
    To call upon a neighbour and to say: –
'We invaded you last night – we are quite prepared to fight,
    Unless you pay us cash to go away.'

And that is called asking for Dane-geld,
    And the people who ask it explain
That you've only to pay 'em the Dane-geld
    And then you'll get rid of the Dane!

It is always a temptation to a rich and lazy nation,
    To puff and look important and to say: –
'Though we know we should defeat you, we have not the time
                       to meet you.
  We will therefore pay you cash to go away.'

And that is called paying the Dane-geld;
    But we've proved it again and again,
That if once you have paid him the Dane-geld
    You never get rid of the Dane.

It is wrong to put temptation in the path of any nation,
    For fear they should succumb and go astray;
So when you are requested to pay up or be molested,
    You will find it better policy to say: –

'We never pay *any*-one Dane-geld,
    No matter how trifling the cost;
For the end of that game is oppression and shame,
    And the nation that plays it is lost!'

# The Glory of the Garden

Our England is a garden that is full of stately views,
Of borders, beds and shrubberies and lawns and avenues,
With statues on the terraces and peacocks strutting by;
But the Glory of the Garden lies in more than meets the eye.

For where the old thick laurels grow, along the thin red wall,
You will find the tool- and potting-sheds which are the heart of
all;
The cold-frames and the hot-houses, the dungpits and the tanks,
The rollers, carts and drain-pipes, with the barrows and the
planks.

And there you'll see the gardeners, the men and 'prentice boys
Told off to do as they are bid and do it without noise;
For, except when seeds are planted and we shout to scare the
birds,
The Glory of the Garden it abideth not in words.

And some can pot begonias and some can bud a rose,
And some are hardly fit to trust with anything that grows;
But they can roll and trim the lawns and sift the sand and loam,
For the Glory of the Garden occupieth all who come.

Our England is a garden, and such gardens are not made
By singing: – 'Oh, how beautiful!' and sitting in the shade,
While better men than we go out and start their working lives
At grubbing weeds from gravel-paths with broken dinner-knives.

There's not a pair of legs so thin, there's not a head so thick,
There's not a hand so weak and white, nor yet a heart so sick,
But it can find some needful job that's crying to be done,
For the Glory of the Garden glorifieth every one.

Then seek your job with thankfulness and work till further orders,
If it's only netting strawberries or killing slugs on borders;
And when your back stops aching and your hands begin to
harden,
You will find yourself a partner in the Glory of the Garden.

Oh, Adam was a gardener, and God who made him sees
That half a proper gardener's work is done upon his knees,
So when your work is finished, you can wash your hands and
pray

For the Glory of the Garden, that it may not pass away!
*And the Glory of the Garden it shall never pass away!*


## 'For All We Have and Are'
### 1914


For all we have and are,
For all our children's fate,
Stand up and take the war,
The Hun is at the gate!
Our world has passed away,
In wantonness o'erthrown.
There is nothing left to-day
But steel and fire and stone!
    Though all we knew depart,
    The old Commandments stand: –
    'In courage keep your heart,
    In strength lift up your hand.'

Once more we hear the word
That sickened earth of old: –
'No law except the Sword
Unsheathed and uncontrolled.'
Once more it knits mankind,
Once more the nations go
To meet and break and bind
A crazed and driven foe.

Comfort, content, delight,
The ages' slow-bought gain,
They shrivelled in a night.
Only ourselves remain
To face the naked days
In silent fortitude,
Through perils and dismays
Renewed and re-renewed.
Though all we made depart,
The old Commandments stand: –
'In patience keep your heart,
In strength lift up your hand.'

No easy hope or lies
Shall bring us to our goal,
But iron sacrifice
Of body, will, and soul.
There is but one task for all –
One life for each to give.
What stands if Freedom fall?
Who dies if England live?


## Gehazi

*1915*


Whence comest thou, Gehazi,
    So reverend to behold,
In scarlet and in ermines
    And chain of England's gold?
'From following after Naaman
    To tell him all is well,
Whereby my zeal hath made me
    A Judge in Israel.'

Well done, well done, Gehazi!
　　Stretch forth thy ready hand.
Thou barely 'scaped from judgment,
　　Take oath to judge the land
Unswayed by gift of money
　　Or privy bribe, more base,
Of knowledge which is profit
　　In any market-place.

Search out and probe, Gehazi,
　　As thou of all canst try,
The truthful, well-weighed answer
　　That tells the blacker lie –
The loud, uneasy virtue,
　　The anger feigned at will,
To overbear a witness
　　And make the Court keep still.

Take order now, Gehazi,
　　That no man talk aside
In secret with his judges
　　The while his case is tried.
Lest he should show them – reason
　　To keep a matter hid,
And subtly lead the questions
　　Away from what he did.

Thou mirror of uprightness,
　　What ails thee at thy vows?
What means the risen whiteness
　　Of the skin between thy brows?
The boils that shine and burrow,
　　The sores that slough and bleed –
The leprosy of Naaman
　　　On thee and all thy seed?
　　　　Stand up, stand up, Gehazi,
　　　　　Draw close thy robe and go,
　　　　Gehazi, Judge in Israel,
　　　　　A leper white as snow!

111

# My Boy Jack

## 1914–18

'Have you news of my boy Jack?'
    *Not this tide.*
'When d'you think that he'll come back?'
    *Not with this wind blowing, and this tide.*

'Has any one else had word of him?'
    *Not this tide.*
*For what is sunk will hardly swim,*
    *Not with this wind blowing, and this tide.*

'Oh, dear, what comfort can I find?'
    *None this tide,*
    *Nor any tide,*
*Except he did not shame his kind –*
    *Not even with that wind blowing, and that tide.*

*Then hold your head up all the more,*
    *This tide,*
    *And every tide;*
*Because he was the son you bore,*
    *And gave to that wind blowing and that tide!*


# The Comforters

*('The Dog Hervey'* – A Diversity of Creatures)

Until thy feet have trod the Road
Advise not wayside folk,
Nor till thy back has borne the Load
Break in upon the broke.

112

Chase not with undesired largesse
    Of sympathy the heart
Which, knowing her own bitterness,
    Presumes to dwell apart.

Employ not that glad hand to raise
    The God-forgotten head
To Heaven and all the neighbours' gaze –
    Cover thy mouth instead.

The quivering chin, the bitten lip,
    The cold and sweating brow,
Later may yearn for fellowship –
    Not now, you ass, not now!

Time, not thy ne'er so timely speech,
    Life, not thy views thereon,
Shall furnish or deny to each
    His consolation.

Or, if impelled to interfere,
    Exhort, uplift, advise,
Lend not a base, betraying ear
    To all the victim's cries.

Only the Lord can understand,
    When those first pangs begin,
How much is reflex action and
    How much is really sin.

E'en from good words thyself refrain,
    And tremblingly admit
There is no anodyne for pain
    Except the shock of it.

So, when thine own dark hour shall fall,
    Unchallenged canst thou say:
'I never worried *you* at all,
    For God's sake go away!'

# A Translation

*('Regulus'– A Diversity of Creatures)*

There are whose study is of smells,
    And to attentive schools rehearse
How something mixed with something else
    Makes something worse.

Some cultivate in broths impure
    The clients of our body – these,
Increasing without Venus, cure,
    Or cause, disease.

Others the heated wheel extol,
    And all its offspring, whose concern
Is how to make it farthest roll
    And fastest turn.

Me, much incurious if the hour
    Present, or to be paid for, brings
Me to Brundusium by the power
    Of wheels or wings;

Me, in whose breast no flame hath burned
    Life-long, save that by Pindar lit,
Such lore leaves cold. I am not turned
    Aside to it

More than when, sunk in thought profound
    Of what the unaltering Gods require,
My steward (friend but slave) brings round
    Logs for my fire.

# The Children

## 1914–18

*('The Honours of War'* – A Diversity of Creatures)

These were our children who died for our lands: they were dear
                                        in our sight.
  We have only the memory left of their home-treasured
                                        sayings and laughter.
  The price of our loss shall be paid to our hands, not another's
                                        hereafter.
Neither the Alien nor Priest shall decide on it. That is our right.
  *But who shall return us the children?*

At the hour the Barbarian chose to disclose his pretences,
  And raged against Man, they engaged, on the breasts that
                                        they bared for us,
  The first felon-stroke of the sword he had long-time prepared
                                        for us –
Their bodies were all our defence while we wrought our
                                        defences.

They bought us anew with their blood, forbearing to blame us,
  Those hours which we had not made good when the Judgment
                                        o'ercame us.
They believed us and perished for it. Our statecraft, our learning
  Delivered them bound to the Pit and alive to the burning
  Whither they mirthfully hastened as jostling for honour –
Not since her birth has our Earth seen such worth loosed upon her!

Nor was their agony brief, or once only imposed on them.
  The wounded, the war-spent, the sick received no exemption:
  Being cured they returned and endured and achieved our
                                        redemption,
Hopeless themselves of relief, till Death, marvelling, closed on
                                        them.

That flesh we had nursed from the first in all cleanness was given
To corruption unveiled and assailed by the malice of Heaven –
By the heart-shaking jests of Decay where it lolled on the wires –
To be blanched or gay-painted by fumes – to be cindered by fires –
To be senselessly tossed and retossed in stale mutilation
From crater to crater. For this we shall take expiation.
*But who shall return us our children?*


# Mine Sweepers

## 1914–18

*(Sea Warfare)*


Dawn off the Foreland – the young flood making
    Jumbled and short and steep –
Black in the hollows and bright where it's breaking –
    Awkward water to sweep.
    'Mines reported in the fairway,
    Warn all traffic and detain.
Sent up *Unity, Claribel, Assyrian, Stormcock,* and *Golden Gain.'*

Noon off the Foreland – the first ebb making
    Lumpy and strong in the bight.
Boom after boom, and the golf-hut shaking
    And the jackdaws wild with fright!
    'Mines located in the fairway,
    Boats now working up the chain,
Sweepers – *Unity, Claribel, Assyrian, Stormcock,* and *Golden Gain.'*

Dusk off the Foreland – the last light going
    And the traffic crowding through,
And five damned trawlers with their syreens blowing
    Heading the whole review!
    'Sweep completed in the fairway.
    No more mines remain.
Sent back *Unity, Claribel, Assyrian, Stormcock,* and *Golden Gain.'*

# The Fabulists

## 1914–18

('The Vortex'– A Diversity of Creatures)

When all the world would keep a matter hid,
  Since Truth is seldom friend to any crowd,
Men write in fable, as old Aesop did,
  Jesting at that which none will name aloud.
And this they needs must do, or it will fall
Unless they please they are not heard at all.

When desperate Folly daily laboureth
  To work confusion upon all we have,
When diligent Sloth demandeth Freedom's death,
  And banded Fear commandeth Honour's grave –
Even in that certain hour before the fall,
Unless men please they are not heard at all.

Needs must all please, yet some not all for need,
  Needs must all toil, yet some not all for gain,
But that men taking pleasure may take heed,
  Whom present toil shall snatch from later pain.
Thus some have toiled, but their reward was small
Since, though they pleased, they were not heard at all.

*This* was the lock that lay upon our lips,
  This was the yoke that we have undergone,
Denying us all pleasant fellowships
  As in our time and generation.
Our pleasures unpursued age past recall,
And for our pains – we are not heard at all.

What man hears aught except the groaning guns?
  What man heeds aught save what each instant brings?
When each man's life all imaged life outruns,
  What man shall pleasure in imaginings?
So it hath fallen, as it was bound to fall,
We are not, nor we were not, heard at all.

# En-dor

## 1914–189–?

*('Behold there is a woman that hath a familiar spirit at En-dor.'*
*I Samuel xxviii, 7)*

The road to En-dor is easy to tread
    For Mother or yearning Wife.
There, it is sure, we shall meet our Dead
    As they were even in life.
Earth has not dreamed of the blessing in store
For desolate hearts on the road to En-dor.

Whispers shall comfort us out of the dark –
    Hands – ah God! – that we knew!
Visions and voices – look and hark! –
    Shall prove that the tale is true,
And that those who have passed to the further shore
May be hailed – at a price – on the road to En-dor.

But they are so deep in their new eclipse
    Nothing they say can reach
Unless it be uttered by alien lips
    And framed in a stranger's speech.
The son must send word to the mother that bore,
Through an hireling's mouth. 'Tis the rule of En-dor.

And not for nothing these gifts are shown
    By such as delight our Dead.
They must twitch and stiffen and slaver and groan
    Ere the eyes are set in the head,
And the voice from the belly begins. Therefore,
We pay them a wage where they ply at En-dor.

Even so, we have need of faith
    And patience to follow the clue.
Often, at first, what the dear one saith
    Is babble, or jest, or untrue.
(Lying spirits perplex us sore
Till our loves – and their lives – are well-known at En-dor) …

118

*Oh, the road to En-dor is the oldest road*
*And the craziest road of all!*
*Straight it runs to the Witch's abode,*
*As it did in the days of Saul,*
*And nothing has changed of the sorrow in store*
*For such as go down on the road to En-dor!*


## Gethsemane

### 1914–18


The Garden called Gethsemane
  In Picardy it was,
And there the people came to see
  The English soldiers pass.
We used to pass – we used to pass
  Or halt, as it might be,
And ship our masks in case of gas
  Beyond Gethsemane.

The Garden called Gethsemane,
  It held a pretty lass,
But all the time she talked to me
  I prayed my cup might pass.
The officer sat on the chair,
  The men lay on the grass,
And all the time we halted there
  I prayed my cup might pass.

It didn't pass – it didn't pass –
  It didn't pass from me.
I drank it when we met the gas
  Beyond Gethsemane!

# The Craftsman

Once, after long-drawn revel at The Mermaid,
He to the overbearing Boanerges
Jonson, uttered (if half of it were liquor,
      Blessed be the vintage!)

Saying how, at an alehouse under Cotswold,
He had made sure of his very Cleopatra,
Drunk with enormous, salvation-contemning
      Love for a tinker.

How, while he hid from Sir Thomas's keepers,
Crouched in a ditch and drenched by the midnight
Dews, he had listened to gipsy Juliet
      Rail at the dawning.

How at Bankside, a boy drowning kittens
Winced at the business; whereupon his sister –
Lady Macbeth aged seven – thrust 'em under,
      Sombrely scornful.

How on a Sabbath, hushed and compassionate –
She being known since her birth to the townsfolk –
Stratford dredged and delivered from Avon
      Dripping Ophelia.

So, with a thin third finger marrying
Drop to wine-drop domed on the table,
Shakespeare opened his heart till the sunrise
      Entered to hear him.

London waked and he, imperturbable,
Passed from waking to hurry after shadows …
Busied upon shows of no earthly importance?
      Yes, but he knew it!

# from *Epitaphs of the War*
## *1914–18*

### *'Equality of Sacrifice'*

A. 'I was a Have.' B. 'I was a "have-not".'
(*Together.*) 'What hast thou given which I gave not?'

### *A Servant*

We were together since the War began.
He was my servant – and the better man.

### *A Son*

My son was killed while laughing at some jest. I would I knew
What it was, and it might serve me in a time when jests are few.

### *The Coward*

I could not look on Death, which being known,
Men led me to him, blindfold and alone.

### *Pelicans in the Wilderness*

#### *A Grave near Halfa*

The blown sand heaps on me, that none may learn
　　Where I am laid for whom my children grieve …
O wings that beat at dawning, ye return
　　Out of the desert to your young at eve!

## The Favour

Death favoured me from the first, well knowing I could not
                                                    endure
  To wait on him day by day. He quitted my betters and came
Whistling over the fields, and, when he had made all sure,
  'Thy line is at an end,' he said, 'but at least I have saved its name.'


## The Beginner

On the first hour of my first day
  In the front trench I fell.
(Children in boxes at a play
  Stand up to watch it well.)


## The Refined Man

I was of delicate mind. I stepped aside for my needs,
  Disdaining the common office. I was seen from afar and killed …
How is this matter for mirth? Let each man be judged by his deeds.
  *I have paid my price to live with myself on the terms that I willed.*


## The Sleepy Sentinel

Faithless the watch that I kept: now I have none to keep.
I was slain because I slept: now I am slain I sleep.
Let no man reproach me again, whatever watch is unkept –
I sleep because I am slain. They slew me because I slept.


## Common Form

If any question why we died,
Tell them, because our fathers lied.

## A Dead Statesman

I could not dig: I dared not rob:
Therefore I lied to please the mob.
Now all my lies are proved untrue
And I must face the men I slew.
What tale shall serve me here among
Mine angry and defrauded young?

## A Drifter Off Tarentum

He from the wind-bitten North with ship and companions
                                        descended,
   Searching for eggs of death spawned by invisible hulls.
Many he found and drew forth. Of a sudden the fishery ended
   In flame and a clamorous breath known to the eye-pecking gulls.

## Unknown Female Corpse

Headless, lacking foot and hand,
Horrible I come to land.
I beseech all women's sons
Know I was a mother once.

# The Gods of the Copybook Headings
## 1919

As I pass through my incarnations in every age and race,
I make my proper prostrations to the Gods of the Market-Place.
Peering through reverent fingers I watch them flourish and fall,
And the Gods of the Copybook Headings, I notice, outlast them
all.

We were living in trees when they met us. They showed us each
in turn
That Water would certainly wet us, as Fire would certainly burn:
But we found them lacking in Uplift, Vision and Breadth of Mind,
So we left them to teach the Gorillas while we followed the
March of Mankind.

We moved as the Spirit listed. *They* never altered their pace,
Being neither cloud nor wind-borne like the Gods of the Market-
Place:
But they always caught up with our progress, and presently
word would come
That a tribe had been wiped off its icefield, or the lights had
gone out in Rome.

With the Hopes that our World is built on they were utterly out
of touch,
They denied that the Moon was Stilton; they denied she was
even Dutch.
They denied that Wishes were Horses; they denied that a Pig
had Wings.
So we worshipped the Gods of the Market Who promised these
beautiful things.

When the Cambrian measures were forming, They promised
perpetual peace.
They swore, if we gave them our weapons, that the wars of the
tribes would cease.
But when we disarmed They sold us and delivered us bound to
our foe,

And the Gods of the Copybook Headings said: '*Stick to the Devil
you know.*'

On the first Feminian Sandstones we were promised the Fuller Life
(Which started by loving our neighbour and ended by loving his
wife)
Till our women had no more children and the men lost reason
and faith,
And the Gods of the Copybook Headings said: '*The Wages of Sin
is Death.*'

In the Carboniferous Epoch we were promised abundance for all,
By robbing selected Peter to pay for collective Paul;
But, though we had plenty of money, there was nothing our
money could buy,
And the Gods of the Copybook Headings said: '*If you don't work
you die.*'

Then the Gods of the Market tumbled, and their smooth-
tongued wizards withdrew,
And the hearts of the meanest were humbled and began to
believe it was true
That All is not Gold that Glitters, and Two and Two make Four –
And the Gods of the Copybook Headings limped up to explain it
once more.

\*

As it will be in the future, it was at the birth of Man –
There are only four things certain since Social Progress began: –
That the Dog returns to his Vomit and the Sow returns to her Mire,
And the burnt Fool's bandaged finger goes wabbling back to the
Fire;

And that after this is accomplished, and the brave new world
begins
When all men are paid for existing and no man must pay for his
sins,
As surely as Water will wet us, as surely as Fire will burn,
The Gods of the Copybook Headings with terror and slaughter
return!

# Chartres Windows
## 1925


Colour fulfils where Music has no power:
　　By each man's light the unjudging glass betrays
All men's surrender, each man's holiest hour
　　And all the lit confusion of our days –
Purfled with iron, traced in dusk and fire,
　　Challenging ordered Time who, at the last,
　　Shall bring it, grozed and leaded and wedged fast,
　　To the cold stone that curbs or crowns desire.
Yet on the pavement that all feet have trod –
　　Even as the Spirit, in her deeps and heights,
Turns only, and that voiceless, to her God –
　　There falls no tincture from those anguished lights.
And Heaven's one light, behind them, striking through
Blazons what each man dreamed no other knew.


# The Changelings

## (R.N.V.R.)

*('Sea Constables'* – Debits and Credits*)*


Or ever the battered liners sank
　　With their passengers to the dark,
I was head of a Walworth Bank,
　　And you were a grocer's clerk.

I was a dealer in stocks and shares,
　　And you in butters and teas;
And we both abandoned our own affairs
　　And took to the dreadful seas.


126

Wet and worry about our ways –
  Panic, onset, and flight –
Had us in charge for a thousand days
  And a thousand-year-long night.

We saw more than the nights could hide –
  More than the waves could keep –
And – certain faces over the side
  Which do not go from our sleep.

We were more tired than words can tell
  While the pied craft fled by,
And the swinging mounds of the Western swell
  Hoisted us Heavens-high …

Now there is nothing – not even our rank –
  To witness what we have been;
And I am returned to my Walworth Bank,
  And you to your margarine!


## To the Companions

*('The United Idolaters' – Debits and Credits)*


How comes it that, at even-tide,
  When level beams should show most truth,
Man, failing, takes unfailing pride
  In memories of his frolic youth?

Venus and Liber fill their hour;
  The games engage, the law-courts prove;
Till hardened life breeds love of power
  Or Avarice, Age's final love.

127

Yet at the end, these comfort not –
Nor any triumph Fate decrees –
Compared with glorious, unforgot-
ten innocent enormities

Of frontless days before the beard,
When, instant on the casual jest,
The God Himself of Mirth appeared
And snatched us to His heaving breast.

And we – not caring who He was
But certain He would come again –
Accepted all He brought to pass
As Gods accept the lives of men ...

Then He withdrew from sight and speech,
Nor left a shrine. How comes it now,
While Charon's keel grates on the beach,
He calls so clear: 'Rememberest thou?'


## Jane's Marriage

*('The Janeites' – Debits and Credits)*


Jane went to Paradise:
    That was only fair.
Good Sir Walter followed her,
    And armed her up the stair.
Henry and Tobias,
    And Miguel of Spain,
Stood with Shakespeare at the top
    To welcome Jane –

Then the Three Archangels
    Offered out of hand
Anything in Heaven's gift
    That she might command.
Azrael's eyes upon her,
    Raphael's wings above,
Michael's sword against her heart,
    Jane said: 'Love.'

Instantly the under-
    standing Seraphim
Laid their fingers on their lips
    And went to look for him.
Stole across the Zodiac,
    Harnessed Charles's Wain,
And whispered round the Nebulae
    'Who loved Jane?'

In a private limbo
    Where none had thought to look,
Sat a Hampshire gentleman
    Reading of a book.
It was called *Persuasion*
    And it told the plain
Story of the love between
    Him and Jane.

He heard the question
    Circle Heaven through –
Closed the book and answered:
    'I did – and do!'
Quietly but speedily
    (As Captain Wentworth moved)
Entered into Paradise
    The man Jane loved!

*Jane lies in Winchester, blessèd be her shade!*
*Praise the Lord for making her, and her for all she made.*
*And, while the stones of Winchester – or Milsom Street – remain,*
*Glory, Love, and Honour unto England's Jane!*

# Gipsy Vans

('*A Madonna of the Trenches*' – Debits and Credits)

Unless you come of the gipsy stock
    That steals by night and day,
Lock your heart with a double lock
    And throw the key away.
Bury it under the blackest stone
    Beneath your father's hearth,
And keep your eyes on your lawful own
    And your feet to the proper path.
        *Then you can stand at your door and mock*
          *When the gipsy vans come through …*
        *For it isn't right that the Gorgio stock*
          *Should live as the Romany do.*

Unless you come of the gipsy blood
    That takes and never spares,
Bide content with your given good
    And follow your own affairs.
Plough and harrow and roll your land,
    And sow what ought to be sowed;
But never let loose your heart from your hand,
    Nor flitter it down the road!
        *Then you can thrive on your boughten food*
          *As the gipsy vans come through …*
        *For it isn't nature the Gorgio blood*
          *Should love as the Romany do.*

Unless you carry the gipsy eyes
    That see but seldom weep,
Keep your head from the naked skies
    Or the stars'll trouble your sleep.
Watch your moon through your window-pane
    And take what weather she brews;
But don't run out in the midnight rain
    Nor home in the morning dews.
        *Then you can huddle and shut your eyes*
          *As the gipsy vans come through …*
        *For it isn't fitting the Gorgio ryes*
          *Should walk as the Romany do.*

Unless you come of the gipsy race
  That counts all time the same,
Be you careful of Time and Place
  And Judgment and Good Name:
Lose your life for to live your life
  The way that you ought to do;
And when you are finished, your God and your wife
  And the Gipsies'll laugh at you!
    *Then you can rot in your burying place*
    *As the gipsy vans come through ...*
    *For it isn't reason the Gorgio race*
    *Should die as the Romany do.*


## We and They

('*A Friend of the Family*' – Debits and Credits)


Father and Mother, and Me,
  Sister and Auntie say
All the people like us are We,
  And every one else is They.
And They live over the sea,
  While We live over the way,
But – would you believe it? – They look upon We
  As only a sort of They!

We eat pork and beef
  With cow-horn-handled knives.
They who gobble Their rice off a leaf,
  Are horrified out of Their lives;
While They who live up a tree,
  And feast on grubs and clay,
(Isn't it scandalous?) look upon We
  As a simply disgusting They!

131

We shoot birds with a gun.
　　They stick lions with spears.
Their full-dress is un-.
　　We dress up to Our ears.
They like Their friends for tea.
　　We like Our friends to stay;
And, after all that, They look upon We
　　As an utterly ignorant They!

We eat kitcheny food.
　　We have doors that latch.
They drink milk or blood,
　　Under an open thatch.
We have Doctors to fee.
　　They have Wizards to pay.
And (impudent heathen!) They look upon We
　　As a quite impossible They!

All good people agree,
　　And all good people say,
All nice people, like Us, are We
　　And every one else is They:
But if you cross over the sea,
　　Instead of over the way,
You may end by (think of it!) looking on We
　　As only a sort of They!

# The Burden

(*'The Gardener'* – Debits and Credits)

One grief on me is laid
    Each day of every year,
Wherein no soul can aid,
    Whereof no soul can hear:
Whereto no end is seen
    Except to grieve again –
Ah, Mary Magdalene,
    Where is there greater pain?

To dream on dear disgrace
    Each hour of every day –
To bring no honest face
    To aught I do or say:
To lie from morn till e'en –
    To know my lies are vain –
Ah, Mary Magdalene,
    Where can be greater pain?

To watch my steadfast fear
    Attend mine every way
Each day of every year –
    Each hour of every day:
To burn, and chill between –
    To quake and rage again –
Ah, Mary Magdalene,
    Where shall be greater pain?

*One grave to me was given –*
    *To guard till Judgment Day –*
*But God looked down from Heaven*
    *And rolled the Stone away!*
*One day of all my years –*
    *One hour of that one day –*
*His Angel saw my tears*
    *And rolled the Stone away!*

# from *The Muse Among the Motors*
## *c.1901–1929*

### *Sepulchral*

*(From the Greek Anthologies)*

Swifter than aught 'neath the sun the car of Simonides moved him.
Two things he could not out-run – Death and a Woman who
loved him.

### *Arterial*

*(Early Chinese)*

#### I

Frost upon small rain – the ebony-lacquered avenue
    Reflecting lamps as a pool shows goldfish.
The sight suddenly emptied out of the young man's eyes
    Entering upon it sideways.

#### II

In youth, by hazard, I killed an old man.
    In age I maimed a little child.
Dead leaves under foot reproach not:
But the lop-sided cherry-branch – whenever the sun rises,
    How black a shadow!

## The Advertisement

*(In the Manner of the Earlier English)*

Whether to wend through straight streets strictly,
Trimly by towns perfectly paved;
Or after office, as fitteth thy fancy,
Faring with friends far among fields;
There is none other equal in action,
Sith she is silent, nimble, unnoisome,
Lordly of leather, gaudily gilded,
Burgeoning brightly in a brass bonnet,
Certain to steer well between wains.

## The Justice's Tale

*(Chaucer)*

With them there rode a lustie Engineere
Wel skilled to handel everich waie her geere,
Hee was soe wise ne man colde showe him naught
And out of Paris was hys learnynge brought.
Frontlings mid brazen wheeles and wandes he sat,
And on hys heade he bare an leathern hat.
Hee was soe certaine of his gouvernance,
That, by the Road, he tooke everie chaunce.
For simple people and for lordlings eke
Hee wolde not bate a del but onlie squeeke
Behinde their backés on an horné hie
Until they crope into a piggestie.
He was more wood than bull in china-shoppe,
And yet for cowes and doggés wolde hee stop,
Not out of Marcie but for Preudence-sake –
Than hys dependaunce ever was hys brake.

## 'When the Journey Was Intended to the City'

### (Milton)

When that with meat and drink they had fulfilled
Not temperately but like him conceived
In monstrous jest at Meudon, whose regale
Stands for exemplar of Gargantuan greed,
In his own name supreme, they issued forth
Beneath new firmaments and stars astray,
Circumvoluminant; nor had they felt
Neither the passage nor the sad effect
Of many cups partaken, till that frost
Wrought on them hideous, and their minds deceived.
Thus choosing from a progeny of roads,
That seemed but were not, one most reasonable,
Of purest moonlight fashioned on a wall,
Thither they urged their chariot whom that flint
Buttressed received, itself unscathed – not they.


## The Tour

### (Byron)

Thirteen as twelve my Murray always took –
    He was a publisher. The new Police
Have neater ways of bringing men to book,
    So Juan found himself before J.P.'s
Accused of storming through that placid nook
    At practically any pace you please.
The Dogberry, and the Waterbury, made
It fifty mile – five pounds. And Juan paid!

## The Idiot Boy

*(Wordsworth)*

He wandered down the mountain grade
   Beyond the speed assigned –
A youth whom Justice often stayed
   And generally fined.

He went alone, that none might know
   If he could drive or steer.
Now he is in the ditch, and Oh!
   The differential gear!

## The Bother

*(Clough)*

Hastily Adam our driver swallowed a curse in the darkness –
Petrol nigh at end and something wrong with a sprocket
Made him speer for the nearest town, when lo! at the cross-ways
Four blank letterless arms the virginal signpost extended.
'Look!' thundered Hugh the Radical. 'This is the England we
                        boast of –
Bland, white-bellied, obese, but utterly useless for business.
They are repainting the signs and have left the job in the middle.
They are repainting the signs and traffic may stop till they've
                        done it,
Which is to say till the son-of-a-gun of a local contractor,
Having laboriously wiped out every name for
Probably thirty miles round, be minded to finish his labour!
Had not the fool the sense to paint out and paint in together?'

Thus, not seeing his speech belied his Radical Gospel
(Which is to paint out the earth and then write 'Damn' on the
                        shutter),
Hugh embroidered the theme imperially and stretched it
From some borough in Wales through our Australian possessions,
Making himself, reformer-wise, a bit of a nuisance
Till, with the help of Adam, we cast him out on the landscape.

## The Moral

*(Author Unknown)*

You mustn't groom an Arab with a file.
  You hadn't ought to tension-spring a mule.
You couldn't push a brumby fifty mile
  And drop him in a boiler-shed to cool.
I'll sling you through six counties in a day.
  I'll hike you up a grade of one in ten.
I am Duty, Law and Order under way,
  I'm the Mentor of banana-fingered men!
I will make you know your left hand from your right.
  I will teach you not to drink about your biz.
I'm the only temperance advocate in sight!
  I am all the Education Act there is!

## The Disciple

*('The Church that Was at Antioch' – Limits and Renewals)*

He that hath a Gospel
  To loose upon Mankind,
Though he serve it utterly –
  Body, soul and mind –
Though he go to Calvary
  Daily for its gain –
It is His Disciple
  Shall make his labour vain.

138

He that hath a Gospel
　　For all earth to own –
Though he etch it on the steel,
　　Or carve it on the stone –
Not to be misdoubted
　　Through the after-days –
It is His Disciple
　　Shall read it many ways.

It is His Disciple
　　(Ere Those Bones are dust)
Who shall change the Charter,
　　Who shall split the Trust –
Amplify distinctions,
　　Rationalise the Claim;
Preaching that the Master
　　Would have done the same.

It is His Disciple
　　Who shall tell us how
Much the Master would have scrapped
　　Had he lived till now –
What he would have modified
　　Of what he said before.
It is His Disciple
　　Shall do this and more …

He that hath a Gospel
　　Whereby Heaven is won
(Carpenter, or cameleer,
　　Or Maya's dreaming son),
Many swords shall pierce Him,
　　Mingling blood with gall;
But His Own Disciple
　　Shall wound Him worst of all!

# The Mother's Son

(*'Fairy Kist'* – Limits and Renewals)

I have a dream – a dreadful dream –
  A dream that is never done.
I watch a man go out of his mind,
  And he is My Mother's Son.

They pushed him into a Mental Home,
  And that is like the grave:
For they do not let you sleep upstairs,
  And you aren't allowed to shave.

And it was *not* disease or crime
  Which got him landed there,
But because They laid on My Mother's Son
  More than a man could bear.

What with noise, and fear of death,
  Waking, and wounds and cold,
They filled the Cup for My Mother's Son
  Fuller than it could hold.

They broke his body and his mind
  And yet They made him live,
And They asked more of My Mother's Son
  Than any man could give.

For, just because he had not died,
  Nor been discharged nor sick,
They dragged it out with My Mother's Son
  Longer than he could stick ...

And no one knows when he'll get well –
  So, there he'll have to be:
And, 'spite of the beard in the looking-glass,
  I know that man is me!

# The Coiner

('*A Naval Mutiny*' – Limits and Renewals)

*To be sung by the unlearned to the tune of 'King John and the Abbot of*
*Canterbury', and by the learned to 'Tempest-a-brewing'.*

Against the Bermudas we foundered, whereby
This Master, that Swabber, yon Bo'sun, and I
(Our pinnace and crew being drowned in the main)
Must beg for our bread through old England again.

For a bite and a sup, and a bed of clean straw,
We'll tell you such marvels as man never saw,
On a Magical Island which no one did spy
Save this Master, that Swabber, yon Bo'sun, and I.

Seven months among Mermaids and Devils and Sprites,
And Voices that howl in the cedars o' nights,
With further enchantments we underwent there.
Good Sirs, 'tis a tale to draw guts from a bear!

'Twixt Dover and Southwark it paid us our way,
Where we found some poor players were labouring a play;
And, willing to search what such business might be,
We entered the yard, both to hear and to see.

One hailed us for seamen and courteous-ly
Did guide us apart to a tavern near by
Where we told him our tale (as to many of late),
And he gave us good cheer, so we gave him good weight.

Mulled sack and strong waters on bellies well lined
With beef and black pudding do strengthen the mind;
And seeing him greedy for marvels, at last
From plain salted truth to flat leasing we passed.

But he, when on midnight our reckoning he paid,
Says, 'Never match coins with a Coiner by trade,
Or he'll turn your lead pieces to metal as rare
As shall fill him this globe, and leave something to spare …'

We slept where they laid us, and when we awoke
'Was a crown or five shillings in every man's poke.
We bit them and rang them, and, finding them good,
We drank to that Coiner as honest men should!

For a cup and a crust, and a truss, etc.


# Neighbours

('*Beauty Spots*' – Limits and Renewals)


The man that is open of heart to his neighbour,
    And stops to consider his likes and dislikes,
His blood shall be wholesome whatever his labour,
    His luck shall be with him whatever he strikes.
The Splendour of Morning shall duly possess him,
    That he may not be sad at the falling of eve.
And, when he has done with mere living – God bless him! –
    A many shall sigh, and one Woman shall grieve!

But he that is costive of soul toward his fellow,
    Through the ways, and the works, and the woes of this life,
Him food shall not fatten, him drink shall not mellow;
    And his innards shall brew him perpetual strife.
His eye shall be blind to God's Glory above him;
    His ear shall be deaf to Earth's Laughter around;
His Friends and his Club and his Dog shall not love him;
    And his Widow shall skip when he goes underground!

# Hymn to Physical Pain

*('The Tender Achilles'* – Limits and Renewals*)*

Dread Mother of Forgetfulness
   Who, when Thy reign begins,
Wipest away the Soul's distress,
   And memory of her sins.

The trusty Worm that dieth not –
   The steadfast Fire also,
By Thy contrivance are forgot
   In a completer woe.

Thine are the lidless eyes of night
   That stare upon our tears,
Through certain hours which in our sight
   Exceed a thousand years:

Thine is the thickness of the Dark
   That presses in our pain,
As Thine the Dawn that bids us mark
   Life's grinning face again.

Thine is the weariness outworn
   No promise shall relieve,
That says at eve 'Would God 'twere morn!'
   At morn 'Would God 'twere eve!'

And when Thy tender mercies cease
   And life unvexed is due,
Instant upon the false release
   The Worm and Fire renew.

Wherefore we praise Thee in the deep,
   And on our beds we pray
For Thy return that Thou may'st keep
   The Pains of Hell at bay!

# The Storm Cone

## 1932

This is the midnight – let no star
Delude us – dawn is very far.
This is the tempest long foretold –
Slow to make head but sure to hold.

Stand by! The lull 'twixt blast and blast
Signals the storm is near, not past;
And worse than present jeopardy
May our forlorn to-morrow be.

If we have cleared the expectant reef,
Let no man look for his relief.
Only the darkness hides the shape
Of further peril to escape.

It is decreed that we abide
The weight of gale against the tide
And those huge waves the outer main
Sends in to set us back again.

They fall and whelm. We strain to hear
The pulses of her labouring gear,
Till the deep throb beneath us proves,
After each shudder and check, she moves!

She moves, with all save purpose lost,
To make her offing from the coast;
But, till she fetches open sea,
Let no man deem that he is free!

# Samuel Pepys
## 1933

Like as the Oak whose roots descend
   Through earth and stillness seeking food
Most apt to furnish in the end
   That dense, indomitable wood

Which, felled, may arm a seaward flank
   Of Ostia's mole or – bent to frame
The beaked Liburnian's triple bank –
   Carry afar the Roman name;

But which, a tree, the season moves
   Through gentler Gods than Wind or Tide,
Delightedly to harbour doves,
   Or take some clasping vine for bride;

So this man – prescient to ensure
   (Since even now his orders hold)
A little State might ride secure
   At sea from foes her sloth made bold –

Turned in his midmost harried round,
   As Venus drove or Liber led,
And snatched from any shrine he found
   The Stolen Draught, the Secret Bread.

Nor these alone. His life betrayed
   No gust unslaked, no pleasure missed.
He talked the obedient Nine to aid
   The varied chase. And Clio kissed;

Bidding him write each sordid love,
   Shame, panic, stratagem, and lie
In full, that sinners undiscov-
   ered, like ourselves, might say: – "Tis I!'

# Hymn of Breaking Strain
## 1935

The careful text-books measure
  (Let all who build beware!)
The load, the shock, the pressure
  Material can bear.
So, when the buckled girder
  Lets down the grinding span
The blame of loss, or murder,
  Is laid upon the man.
    *Not on the Stuff – the Man!*

But, in our daily dealing
  With stone and steel, we find
The Gods have no such feeling
  Of justice toward mankind.
To no set gauge they make us –
  For no laid course prepare –
And presently o'ertake us
  With loads we cannot bear:
    *Too merciless to bear.*

The prudent text-books give it
  In tables at the end –
The stress that shears a rivet
  Or make a tie-bar bend –
What traffic wrecks macadam –
  What concrete should endure –
But we, poor sons of Adam,
  Have no such literature.
    *To warn us or make sure!*

We hold all Earth to plunder –
  All Time and Space as well –
Too wonder-stale to wonder
  At each new miracle;
Till, in the mid-illusion
  Of Godhead 'neath our hand,
Falls multiple confusion
  On all we did or planned –
    *The mighty works we planned.*

We only of Creation
  *(Oh, luckier bridge and rail!)*
Abide the twin damnation –
  To fail and know we fail.
Yet we – by which sole token
  We know we once were Gods –
Take shame in being broken
  However great the odds –
    *The Burden or the Odds.*

Oh, veiled and secret Power
  Whose paths we seek in vain,
Be with us in our hour
  Of overthrow and pain;
That we – by which sure token
  We know Thy ways are true –
In spite of being broken,
  *Because of being broken,*
    *May rise and build anew.*
    *Stand up and build anew!*

# Notes

**Credat Judaeus**. Written at school at Westward Ho! when Kipling was just fifteen. *Credat Judaeus*: see Horace, *Satires* I:5. In his invaluable notes to *Early Verse by Rudyard Kipling 1879–1889* (OUP, 1986), Andrew Rutherford neatly glosses the phrase 'Credat Judaeus' as 'Tell it to the marines'.

**An Auto-da-Fé**. Dated 3 November 1881. *Auto-da-Fé*: literally, the public burning of a heretic by the Inquisition; here the burning of Kipling's love letters and poems to Flo Garrard, with whom he continued to be unhappily in love for many years.

**Donec Gratus Eram**. A free translation into Devonshire dialect of Horace, *Odes* 3:9; written in 1882 at Westward Ho! Together with 'Credat Judaeus', the poem offers early evidence of Kipling's lifelong admiration for Horace (see the note to 'A Translation').

**Ave Imperatrix!**. Modelled on Oscar Wilde's 'Ave Imperatrix' (though without Wilde's republican ending). *Ave Imperatrix!*: Hail Empress.

**The Pious Sub's Creed**. Dated 26 January 1883. *Sub*: sub-editor; Kipling had recently joined the staff of the *Civil and Military Gazette* in Lahore. *Peshin*: on the North-West Frontier; *Wheeler*: Kipling's editor at the *CMG*, whom he nicknamed the 'Amber Toad'; *gup*: gossip; *babu*: an educated Bengali; *The Indian Civil List*: the official publication listing government officials and posts.

**A Vision of India**. Parody of Part 4 of Tennyson's 'Vision of Sin', first published in *Echoes* (1884), an anonymous volume of parodies put out by Kipling and his sister Trix. *Shake the sere Pagoda-tree*: get rich quick (a pagoda was a southern Indian coin); *degchies*: cooking pots.

**The Flight of the Bucket**. Parody of Robert Browning, published in *Echoes*. *Sordello*: Browning's famously difficult poem; *liquor vitae*: fluid of life; *Lawson*: a Radical Liberal politician in favour of prohibition; *the scrap o' blue at buttonhole*: the blue ribbon worn by temperance supporters.

**Jane Smith**. Parody of Wordsworth's 'Alice Fell', published in *Echoes*, perhaps a collaboration with Trix.

**The Vision of Hamid Ali**. *Ganja*: marijuana; *chillam*: hookah; *the Twelve*: the twelve religious leaders of the Shia branch of Islam; *Moulvie*: title bestowed on the learned; *Roum*: presumably Rome; *khashi*: fresco; *The Banner*: Shiite banner carried at Muharram festival; *the Crescent*: the emblem of Islam; *the Wheel*: the Buddhist emblem of Life; *Parvati*: the Hindu goddess of beauty.

**Of Birthdays**. Sonnet to celebrate Kipling's father's forty-ninth birthday, 6 July 1886; *a childhood desolate*: probably a reference to the traumatising years (1871–7) after the six-year-old Kipling and his even younger sister were sent back from India to England to live with a family in Southsea. Kipling later dubbed the Southsea house the 'House of Desolation'.

**The Story of Uriah**. See 2 Samuel 11 where King David, desiring Bathsheba, arranges for her husband Uriah to be killed in battle. Kipling's poem is said to be based on a contemporary incident. *Quetta*: a city now in West Pakistan.

**A Code of Morals**. *'Dash dot dot, dot, dot dash, dot dash dot'*: 'dear' in Morse code.

**The Man Who Could Write**. *Boanerges Blitzen*: joke name for a journalist, derived from Boanerges ('the sons of thunder', Jesus' collective nickname for James and John, the sons of Zebedee, see Mark 3:17) and 'Blitzen' (the German for 'lightning'); *Ithuriel*: see *Paradise Lost* 4, 788–864 where Ithuriel is one of two guardian angels deputed to protect Adam and Eve. They discover Satan, whispering at Eve's ear, in the form of a toad. Touched by Ithuriel's spear, Satan is forced to resume his 'own likeness' – 'for no falsehood can endure / Touch of celestial temper'. Kipling's journalist sees himself as a would-be Ithuriel (i.e. unmasker of the truth).

**My Rival**. According to Trix, she and her brother composed the poem extempore line for line on the Mall in Simla in the summer of 1885. The ages of speaker and rival exactly correspond to those of Trix and her mother Alice, suggesting a family tease at Alice's expense.

**La Nuit Blanche**. *Tara Devi, Jakko*: hills at Simla.

**Arithmetic on the Frontier**. *"All flesh is grass"*: Isaiah 40:6; *jekail*: Afghan musket.

**One Viceroy Resigns**. *Lord Dufferin* and *Lord Lansdowne*: Viceroys of India (1884–8, 1888–93); *khitmutgars*: butlers; *Colvin* and *Lyall*: Anglo-Indian administrators; *Roberts*: probably Lord Roberts ('Bobs'); *Crosthwaite, Reay, Buck, Westland, Wilson, Hope, Aitchison, Hunter and Marshal*: presumably other Anglo-Indian administrators.

**Inscription on Copy of** *Plain Tales from the Hills*. *Mrs Hill*: American wife of Professor Alexander Hill of the Muir Central College. Kipling was in love with her.

**The Winners**. *Gehenna*: hell.

**Danny Deever**. First of the 'Barrack-Room Ballads', published in W.E. Henley's *Scots Observer* in 1890 and cementing Kipling's early reputation in England. 'Tommy', 'The Widow at Windsor', 'Gunga Din', 'Mandalay' and 'The Young British Soldier' also appeared in this first series.

**Tommy**. *Tommy*: short for Thomas Atkins, generic name for a British Army private, dating back to the Napoleonic wars.

**Gunga Din**. *Bhisti*: water-carrier; *Panee lao*: water, quick: *Harry By*: O brother; *juldee*: be quick; *mussick*: water-skin bag; *dooli*: stretcher.

**The Last of the Light Brigade**. A kind of sequel to Tennyson's 'The Charge of the Light Brigade'. Kipling's point seems to be that Tennyson should have written a follow-up poem to raise money for the destitute survivors of the charge, but didn't.

**Tomlinson**. *Empusa's crew*: hobgoblins sent by Hecate.

**The Long Trail**. *The Tents of Shem*: see Genesis 9:27 – here Kipling's shorthand for the rat-race; *the Peter*: Blue Peter flag, hoisted to indicate a ship is about to sail; *the Mouse, the Gull Light*: navigation lights.

**McAndrew's Hymn**. Another of Kipling's Browningesque dramatic monologues, a kind of contemporary version of 'Caliban on Setebos', in which the engineer McAndrew derives his 'natural theology' from his machines. Recalling a recitation of the poem, Conan Doyle was impressed by Kipling's 'dramatic power which enabled him to sustain the Glasgow accent throughout, so that the angular Scottish greaser simply walked the room'. Kipling wrote a companion piece the following year called 'The *Mary Gloster*'. *John Calvin*: originator of the idea that some are predestined to be saved, others to be damned; *The Sin against the Holy Ghost*: the despair that leads to suicide; *Gay Street*: red-light area; *Apollyon*: the Devil as destroyer; *Pelagian*: one who believes the human will is capable of good with the aid of divine grace.

**The Song of the Banjo**. *Broadwood*: a make of piano; *Song of Roland*: *Chanson de Roland*, an eleventh-century Old French poem commemorating the heroic last stand of some of Charlemagne's knights at Roncesvalles in the Pyrennees.

**'For to Admire'**. *Hum deckty hai!*: I'm looking out.

**Sestina of the Tramp-Royal**. *Sestina*: an unrhymed poetic form made up of six six-line stanzas with a three-line envoi, in which the last word of each line is repeated in a different order in each of the stanzas and the envoi.

**Recessional**. Written as a response to all the pomp and imperial self-congratulation accompanying Queen Victoria's Diamond Jubilee in June 1897, and intended, Kipling later claimed, as 'a *nuzzur-wattu* (an averter of the Evil Eye)'. *Recessional*: a hymn sung while the clergy and choir retire after the service; *Nineveh*: sacked by the Medes in 612 BC; *Tyre*: captured by Muslims in 1291; *lesser breeds without the Law*: probably the Germans (but whoever is meant the superior tone is out of place in a poem professing humility and appealing for a suspension of divine judgement).

*from* **Verses on Games**. *Jorrocks, Pigg, Binjimin, Artaxerxes*: sporting characters in R.S. Surtees' *Handley Cross* (1843) etc., much beloved by Kipling. *Coaching*: an alternative, uncollected version of these lines goes: 'Youth on the box and liquor in the boot,/My Lord drives out with My Lord's prostitute.'

**The White Man's Burden**. Published 4 February 1899, two days before the USA decided to take control of the Philippines. Intended as a warning about the rigours of imperial responsibility, the poem has come to exemplify the condescending, infantalising attitudes of coloniser to colonised.

**The Absent-Minded Beggar**. Written in October 1899 (with a setting by Arthur Sullivan) to raise money for the dependants of troops going to the Boer War, the fund eventually closing at £250,000. The title was translated into Italian as 'the distracted mendicant'. *Paul*: Paul Kruger, the Boer leader.

**The Islanders**. *Then ye returned to your trinkets, then ye contented your souls/With the flannelled fools at the wicket or the muddied oafs at the goals*: among other targets, Kipling was here having a dig at the upper-class country-house group known as the 'Souls'. To a Scottish colonel, who objected that the second line was a bit rough on cricketers and footballers, Kipling replied: 'Possibly, but ... [y]ou have to hit an Englishmen more than once on the jaw before he will take a thing seriously.'

*from* **Just So Verses**. The *Just So Stories* was originally made up to entertain Kipling's elder (and extremely inquisitive) daughter Josephine, who died in 1899 aged six. The second part of 'Merrow Down' is clearly an elegy for her.

**Lichtenberg**. *Lichtenberg*: in South Africa.

**A Song to Mithras**. *Mithras*: Persian god of the sun and war, who became a popular deity amongst Roman soldiers from the second century AD.

**A Smuggler's Song**. *Valenciennes*: eighteenth-century lace from the northern French town.

**The Sons of Martha**. See Luke 10:38–42. 'The Sons of Martha' was Kipling's shorthand term for the unacknowledged and unthanked ones who do the work, including waiting on 'the Sons of Mary'.

**The Looking-Glass**. *Queen Mary*: Mary, Queen of Scots, Queen Elizabeth I's prisoner for eighteen years, beheaded in 1587; *Lord Leicester*: Robert Dudley, one of Elizabeth's chief favourites.

**If –**. See the last three quatrains of Donne's 'The Undertaking'. Rather than as a catalogue of wholesome pieties, Kipling's poem should perhaps be seen as an adaptation or imitation of Donne's – the child, like the lover being faced by a set of impossible conditions. In his autobiography *Something of Myself*, Kipling wryly commented that 'If –' 'contained counsels of perfection most easy to give' and that it had been 'anthologized to weariness'.

**Eddi's Service**. *Eddi*: Eddius Stephanius, biographer of St Wilfrid, a leading seventh-century English churchman.

**The Female of the Species**. Written as a response to the Suffragette movement.

**'For All We Have and Are'**. Written almost immediately after the outbreak of the First World War.

**Gehazi**. See 2 Kings 5. Kipling casts Sir Isaac Rufus, Lord Chief Justice of England and at the time widely thought to be implicated in the Marconi Scandal (1912), in the role of Gehazi, Elisha's greedy servant. He then punishes him with the leprosy Elisha inflicted on Gehazi.

**My Boy Jack**. Kipling's only son John was killed on his first day in action at Loos in September 1915.

**A Translation**. This became 'Ode 3' of a spoof fifth book of Horace's odes invented by Kipling and a group of Latinist friends towards the end of the First World War and published as *Q. Horati Flacci Carminum Liber Quintus A Rudyardo et Carolo Graves Anglice Redditus* in 1920. Charles Carrington gives the best account of the spoof in his privately printed *Kipling's Horace* (1978), in which he also assembles fifty-five of Kipling's uncollected Horatian epigrams, squibs and free translations. Kipling continued to write occasional 'odes' from the imaginary Book 5; four of these appeared in *Debits and Credits* (1926).

**En-dor**. Written in early 1918 as a rejection of spiritualist offers (probably from his sister Trix) to contact his dead son John.

**Gethsemane**. See Matthew 26:39, Mark 14:36, Luke 22:42.

**The Craftsman**. Written in impressionistic Sapphics, probably as an offshoot of Kipling's Horatian experiments, but a reminder too of his early admiration for Swinburne, who wrote a number of poems in Sapphics. This is one of several imaginative reconstructions by Kipling of the raw materials that might lie behind Shakespeare's plays (see also the notes to 'The Coiner' and 'The Man Who Could Write').

**The Gods of the Copybook Headings**. The poem is an example of what C.H. Sisson describes as Kipling's desire in his poetry to make 'the irrefutable prose statement'. *Copybook*: literally, a book with examples of handwriting for beginners to copy – hence 'the Gods of the Copybook Headings' here offer a mug's guide to basic, unchanging truths about life; *We moved as the Spirit listeth*: see John 3:8; *the Cambrian measures*: earliest geological period of the Palaeozoic era; *Feminian Sandstones*: spoof geological period, a dig at the Suffragette movement; *the Carboniferous Epoch*: a later geological period of the Palaeozoic era; *brave new world*: see *The Tempest* 5, 5, 183.

**The Changelings**. *R.N.V.R.*: Royal Naval Volunteer Reserve; *pied craft*: literally, parti-coloured, variegated (hence camouflaged?) boats.

**To the Companions**. One of the later occasional 'odes' from the imaginary fifth book of Horace odes.

**Jane's Marriage**. *Sir Walter*: Walter Scott; *Henry*: Henry Fielding; *Tobias*: Tobias Smollett; *Miguel*: Miguel de Cervantes.

**Gipsy Vans**. *Giorgio*: the Romany word for a non-Gipsy; *ryes*: the Romany word for 'gentlemen'.

**The Burden**. See Matthew 28:2, Mark 16:3–4, Luke 24:2, John 20:1.

*from* **The Muse Among the Motors**. The complete sequence of 'The Muse Among the Motors' amounts to twenty-six parodies, written between c.1901 and 1929. An initial set of fourteen (including the spoofs of medieval alliterative verse, Chaucer, Byron and Wordsworth) appeared in the *Daily Mail* in February 1904. By 1919 another six had been added (including the spoofs of Milton, Clough and Author Unknown (Kipling himself)), and by 1929 a further half-dozen (including the spoofs of 'The Greek Anthologies' and 'Early Chinese').

**The Coiner**. A playful reconstruction of the possible real-life experience that might lie behind parts of Shakespeare's *The Tempest*. Kipling had first posited a version of this idea in a letter to the *Spectator* on 2 July 1898. He himself was famous for 'pumping' chance acquaintances in just this manner.

**The Hymn to Physical Pain**. For the last twenty years of his life, Kipling suffered chronic pain from an undiagnosed duodenal ulcer (the perforation of which eventually killed him).

**Samuel Pepys**. *Ostia's mole*: a huge waterbreak at the mouth of the Tiber; *The beaked Liburnian's triple bank*: a trireme; *Clio*: the muse of History.

**The Hymn of Breaking Strain**. Written in late 1933, originally for a masonic-style graduation ceremony for Canadian engineers. Kipling offered the following explanation of the final verse to one of the ceremony's founders: 'not only in spite of being broken, but through being broken (and also taught humility etc.) a man may start again on his job.'

154

# Fyfield*Books*

*Two millennia of essential classics*

The extensive Fyfield*Books* list includes

For more information, including a full list of Fyfield*Books* and a contents list for each title, and details of how to order the books in the UK, visit the Fyfield website at www.fyfieldbooks.co.uk or email info@fyfieldbooks.co.uk. For information about Fyfield*Books* available in the United States and Canada, visit the Routledge website at www.routledge-ny.com.